C I T Y P A C K
London

By Louise Nicholson

2ND EDITION

Fodor's Travel Publications, Inc.
New York • Toronto • London • Sydney • Auckland

WWW.FODORS.COM/

Contents

About this book

KEY TO SYMBOLS

✚	map reference on the fold-out map accompanying this book (see below)	🚌	nearest bus route
✉	address	⛴	nearest riverboat or ferry stop
☎	telephone number	♿	facilities for visitors with disabilities
🕐	opening times	✋	admission charge
🍴	restaurant or café on premises or nearby	↔	other nearby places of interest
Ⓜ	nearest metro (underground) train station	❓	tours, lectures, or special events
🚆	nearest overground train station	➤	indicates the page where you will find a fuller description
		ℹ	tourist information

Citypack London is divided into six sections to cover the six most important aspects of your visit to London. It includes:

- The author's view of the city and its people
- Itineraries, walks and excursions
- The top 25 sights to visit—as selected by the author
- Features on what makes the city special
- Detailed listings of restaurants, hotels, shops and nightlife
- Practical information

In addition, easy-to-read side panels provide extra facts and snippets, highlights of places to visit, and invaluable practical advice.

CROSS-REFERENCES

To help you make the most of your visit, cross-references, indicated by ➤, show you where to find additional information about a place or subject.

MAPS

- **The fold-out map** in the wallet at the back of the book is a comprehensive street plan of London. All the map references given in the book refer to this map. For example, the Wallace Collection, in Manchester Square, has the following information: ✚ E5—indicating the grid square of the map in which the Wallace Collection will be found.

- **The city-center maps** found on the inside front and back covers of the book itself are for quick reference. They show the Top 25 Sights, described on pages 24–48, which are clearly plotted by number (**1** – **25**, not page number) from west to east across the city.

PRICES

Where appropriate, an indication of the cost of an establishment is given by **£** signs: **£££** denotes higher prices, **££** denotes average prices, while **£** denotes lower charges.

LONDON
life

5

INTRODUCING LONDON

Some people claim they know London. They cannot possibly. The joy of this city is that it can never be known. You could live here for 20 years or more and still be a beginner, familiar with some parts, baffled by others.

The stimulus of London is that there is always somewhere left to explore, something new to learn, some dynamic change afoot. Just when you think you have got to grips with it, the great city surprises and confronts you, turning all assumptions upside-down. A new building will change a

view, such as the one across the river from Greenwich after the arrival of the shining shaft of Canary Wharf Tower. Familiar pictures will disappear, at the annual rehang in the Tate Gallery for example, and a feast of new canvases will come into view. Whole areas will change their mood, as Soho has done since the mid-1980s, its friendly seediness transformed into squeaky clean trendiness.

Canary Wharf and Canary Wharf Tower, Docklands

London is a fast city. It buzzes by day and night. Londoners tend to be busy, in a rush, independent. What for them is the enjoyable anonymity of a city can be tough for visitors to deal with, particularly since the climate does not encourage a café society for much of the year. But take a deep breath and join in London life at London's pace, and you will find that they are much more friendly than expected.

London is also an expensive city. But Londoners know how to get the most out of it—from the parks, the churches with free music, the great free national museums, and traditional events

with their parades and colors, to Travelcards, plenty of cheap theater deals, and much, much more. London on a budget need not restrict you.

London is in an administrative muddle. For a city that was once the powerful capital of an efficiently run empire stretching round the world, London today is in an astounding mess. It has no central city administration, no properly co-ordinated public transportation, and too many cars. And yet London has its own order. This city is rare in being truly cosmopolitan and the political, economic and cultural capital of the country. Its citizens share the rhythm of the seasons in the great parks. They share in the annual round of tradition and culture. I still walk in St. James's Park at daffodil time, line up for cheap concert tickets at the Proms, and join Italians at their July festival in Clerkenwell.

London has it all, whatever you want. Simply take London and make of it what you wish.

A floodlit Tower Bridge silhouettes the Waterfall sculpture in Tower Bridge Piazza

The Thames

"The old river on its broad reach unrolled at the decline of day, after ages of good service done to the race that people its bank, spread out in the tranquil dignity of a waterway leading to the uttermost ends of the earth… What greatness had not floated on the ebb of that river into the mystery of an unknown earth… the dreams of men, the seed of commonwealth, the germs of empires." – Joseph Conrad, *Heart of Darkness*

7

LONDON IN FIGURES

CITY SITE
- The capital of England and Great Britain, founded by the Romans in A.D. 43 as a trading port on the River Thames, 40 miles inland from the North Sea

- London is really two cities. The City of London has its origins in the Roman port and is still the commercial center. The City of Westminster, founded a thousand years later 2½ miles upstream, has always been the royal, political and religious center

GREEN PLACES
- Greater London covers 625 square miles, of which 11 percent comprises 1,700 parks

LANGUAGES & NATIONALITIES
- Almost 200 languages are spoken in London. About 30 percent of Londoners were born elsewhere. English is the predominant language, followed by Bengali and then Turkish, the Chinese languages, Gujarati, Urdu, Punjabi, Arabic, and Spanish

ECONOMY
- London's principal industries are retailing, the public sector and tourism, followed by banking, insurance, transportation, communications, and manufacturing

TOURISTS
- There are 15.2 million overseas and 10.9 million British visitors to London a year

- The top attractions are the British Museum, the National Gallery, Madame Tussaud's, the Tower of London, and the Tate Gallery

POPULATION
- During the 16th century, London was Europe's fastest-growing city; its population rose from 75,000 to 200,000

- By 1700, London was Europe's biggest and wealthiest city, with about 700,000 people

- London continued to grow, from under 1 million in 1800 to 6.5 million by 1900, peaking in the 1930s and 1940s at 10 million

- The population has now fallen to 6.8 million

LONDON PEOPLE

SIR NORMAN FOSTER

Foster's avid love of flying anything from sailplanes to light aircraft gives him a bird's-eye view of buildings old and new. Architect of the Sackler Galleries at the Royal Academy, Stansted Airport, and the I.T.N. building in Gray's Inn road, Norman Foster trained in Britain and the U.S. and has designed award-winning buildings all over the world. It is Foster and Partners who will transform the British Museum once the British Library is relocated, and they who will build the pedestrian bridge over the Thames from Bankside to St. Paul's.

SIR TERENCE CONRAN

Synonymous with the shopping revolution of the 1970s, when he founded the Habitat chain, Conran remains a pioneer. His Conran stores sell good design at affordable prices. He has also opened a clutch of successful restaurants, including the vast Quaglino's and Mezzo. The heart of Conran's empire is Butler's Wharf, where the Blue Print café sits above his Design Museum, near three more restaurants.

FRANK BRUNO

Franklin Roy Bruno began his boxing career with the Wandsworth Boys Club in 1970 when he was nine. He turned professional in 1982, has had over 30 victories and finally, on his third attempt, claimed a world heavyweight title in 1995, defeating American Oliver McCall in London. His bluff and down-to-earth sense of humor has won him a place in the affections of the capital, and he has acted in children's theater and on TV.

VIVIENNE WESTWOOD

Britain's brightest and wackiest clothes designer maintains a prominent place in the fashion avant-garde. While in the King's Road, she created punk street style, but after fashion shows such as "Witches and Hypnos" she moved upscale to Mayfair. Here she continues to be crazily imaginative and, despite claims to anarchy, has entered the staid pages of *Who's Who*.

The Governor of H.M. The Tower of London

The Governor of H.M. The Tower of London lives in a house on Tower Green and is in local command of the Tower and its 150 or so residents. The current Governor, Major-General Geoffrey Field, is not only responsible for the Crown Jewels and running the Tower; he is actively committed to revitalizing the surrounding area and may well realize his dream of flooding the Tower's moat.

Vivienne Westwood

9

A CHRONOLOGY

A.D. 43	Emperor Claudius invades Britain; a deep-water port, Londinium, is soon established
200	The Romans put a wall around Londinium, now capital of Britannia Superior; they withdraw in 410
1042	Edward the Confessor becomes king, making London capital of England and Westminster his home; begins the abbey-church of St. Peter
1066	The Norman king, William the Conqueror, defeats King Harold at the Battle of Hastings; begins the Tower of London
1176	Peter de Colechurch builds London's first stone bridge, London Bridge
1477	William Caxton publishes the first book printed in England, on his presses at Westminster
1485	Tudor rule begins, ending 1603; London is Europe's fastest-growing city
1529	Cardinal Thomas Wolsey fails to win Henry VIII a divorce and falls from favor
1531	Inigo Jones designs London's first square, Covent Garden Piazza
1533	Henry VIII breaks with Rome to marry Anne Boleyn; establishes the Church of England
1649	Charles I is executed in Whitehall; the Commonwealth (1649–53) and Protectorate (1653–59) govern England until Charles II is restored to the throne in 1660
1666	The Great Fire of London. Sir Christopher Wren begins St. Paul's Cathedral in 1675
1694	William Paterson founds the Bank of England to fund William and Mary's war with France
1759	The British Museum, London's first public museum, opens

1800–1900	London's population grows from 1 million to 6.5 million; 14 Thames bridges are built 1811–1817 and 15 railroad stations 1836–1874
1802	London becomes the world's largest port
1816–28	John Nash lays out Regent Street, Regent's Park and Regent's Canal
1834	The Palace of Westminster burns down; the new building is almost complete by 1847; the Clock Tower ("Big Ben") is finished in 1858
1837	Queen Victoria begins her 64-year reign
1851	The Great Exhibition is held in Hyde Park
1863	World's first urban underground train service, the Metropolitan Railway, opens. In 1890 the first Tube train runs on the Northern Line
1922	First daily wireless (radio) program broadcast from Savoy Hill; B.B.C. established 1927, first broadcasts in 1936 from Alexandra Palace
1939–45	Blitz bombings destroy a third of the City of London and much of the docks
1951	Festival of Britain held on the site of the South Bank arts complex
1960s	The Beatles, Carnaby Street and the King's Road help create "swinging London"
1980s	As a result of post-war conservation movements, 30,000 London buildings and 300 London areas are now protected by law
1981	Government-backed London Docklands Development Corporation (LDDC) begins the revitalization of the docklands
1994	First Eurostar trains travel through the Channel Tunnel between London and Paris
2000	National Millennium Exhibition, Greenwich

PEOPLE & EVENTS FROM HISTORY

QUEEN BOUDICCA

In A.D. 62, when the widowed Boudicca, Queen of the Iceni in Norfolk, found herself insulted, dispossessed and flogged by the Roman Procurator, she and her people revolted. They sacked Colchester, then marched on London while its governor was away. The thriving city was plundered and laid waste. In 1902 Thomas Thorneycroft immortalized the heroine Queen and her daughters in his bronze on Westminster Bridge.

Statue of Boudicca on Westminster Bridge

SIR HUGH MYDDELTON

The statue of a Tudor aristocrat in doublet and hose stands on Islington Green. This is Sir Hugh Myddelton, a wealthy Welsh goldsmith who became jeweler to James I. Recognizing the lack of good fresh water in the city, he cut a channel from the River Lea, 40 miles away in Hertfordshire, which brought fresh water directly into London —for which he was rewarded with a baronetcy.

JOHN NASH

John Nash created theatrical, stucco-fronted architectural designs. From 1811 onwards, backed by the Prince Regent (later George IV), he gave London its first large-scale unified plan. The great sweep of Regent Street from St. James's Park through Portland Place to Regent's Park emulated Paris in its order and grandeur.

SIR JOSEPH BAZALGETTE

As the population of London grew, so did the amount of sewage pouring into the Thames, until in summer it was known as the Great Stink. Bazalgette solved the problem by building the 3½-mile Victoria Embankment (1864–1874). It incorporates a trunk sewer, underground railroad and flood wall, and is topped by a road, riverside walk and Embankment Gardens.

The Great Fire of London

The fire that broke out at a baker's near Pudding Lane on the night of September 2nd, 1666, was the worst of many fires around that time. Raging for four days and nights, it destroyed four-fifths of the City and 13,200 homes. Sir Christopher Wren, grand architect of the consequent rebuilding of London, designed St. Paul's Cathedral, 51 churches (23 still stand), and the Monument to the tragic fire.

LONDON
how to organize your time

13

ITINERARIES

Walking is the best way to get under London's skin. Using the map, select an area and simply explore. Here are four ideas—but do wander off down an alleyway or into an old shop or a church if you see something intriguing.

ITINERARY ONE	**EARLY LONDON: THE CITY**
	It is best to walk around the City on a weekday
Breakfast	Hearty breakfast at a Smithfield pub (➤ 64)
Morning	St. Bartholomew-the-Great (➤ 46)
	Walk through the medieval side streets to the Museum of London (➤ 47)
	Roman wall in the Barbican and Noble Street
	Goldsmith's Hall and Foster Lane
	Walk along Cheapside, down Bow Lane, and left up Queen Victoria Street
Lunch	Lunch at Sweetings seafood restaurant (➤ 63)
Afternoon	Temple of Mithras, Bucklersbury (➤ 60)
	St. Margaret, Lothbury (➤ 55)
	Guildhall: huge medieval crypt, Clockmakers' Company clocks 🕒 Mon–Fri 9:30–4:45 ✋ Free
ITINERARY TWO	**CHIC LONDON: ST. JAMES'S**
	Especially good for art galleries; best Mon–Fri
Morning	Jermyn Street (➤ 70), then St. James's Square and King Street (Spinks and Christie's ➤ 72)
	St. James's Palace, where the Changing of the Guard begins (➤ 22)
	Up St. James's Street and into St. James's Place to Spencer House (🕒 Sun only; not Jan, Aug)
	Through the tunnel to Queen's Walk by Green Park (➤ 56). Stop for a picnic lunch or:
Lunch	Café Torino, 189 Piccadilly (🕒 Daily)
Afternoon	Walk along Piccadilly, delving into the Ritz, Fortnum & Mason, and Hatchards (➤ 76)
	St. James's Church (➤ 55)
	The Royal Academy (➤ 51)
	Through Burlington Arcade to Cork Street art galleries (➤ 72)
	Bond Street, New and Old (➤ 70); Sotheby's (➤ 72)

ITINERARY THREE	ROYAL LONDON

Choose a dry day on which to alternate parks and picnics with palaces and palatial houses

Morning
Kensington Palace and Kensington Gardens (► 25)
Hyde Park (► 56)
Apsley House (► 52)
Green Park (► 56)
Buckingham Palace (the Queen's Gallery is the part most likely to be open ► 32)

Lunch
Picnic lunch in St. James's Park (► 33)

Afternoon
Horse Guards through to Banqueting House (► 37)
Parliament Square, filled with statues of past prime ministers
The Houses of Parliament (► 36)
Westminster Abbey, where there may be afternoon Evensong (► 35)

ITINERARY FOUR	LONDON, CAPITAL OF AN EMPIRE

You will need to use some public transportation on this walk

Morning
St. Paul's Cathedral (► 45): public statues and memorials in St. Paul's and the streets around. Take bus no. 11, 15, or 23 to Trafalgar Square, dedicated to Nelson and sea heroes (► 53)
National Portrait Gallery (► 38)
Walk down The Mall, laid out as a processional route for Queen Victoria. There's a triumphal arch at one end and her memorial at the other, set in a circle symbolizing the Empress at the heart of her empire

Lunch
Dip into St. James's Park for lunch (► 33)

Afternoon
Take the Underground (District or Circle line) from St. James's Park to High Street Kensington or the no. 9 bus from Trafalgar Square via Hyde Park Corner to Kensington High Street
Pay a visit to the museum in artist Linley Sambourne's former home at 8 Stafford Terrace, or to Leighton House (► 52)

WALKS

THE SIGHTS

- Tower Bridge Museum
  (➤ 57)
- Design Museum (➤ 50)
- Bramah Tea and Coffee
  Museum, Clove Building,
  Maguire Street, SE1
  ☎ 0171 378 0222
- H.M.S. *Belfast* (➤ 58)
- The London Dungeon
  (➤ 58)
- The Clink Exhibition, 1 Clink
  Street, SE1 ☎ 0171 403
  6515 ⊙ Daily 10–6
- Shakespeare Globe Museum,
  New Globe Walk, Bankside,
  SE1 ☎ 0171 928 6406
  ⊙ Daily 10–5
- South Bank Arts Complex
  (➤ 11, 51, and 80)
- London Aquarium (➤ 51)

INFORMATION

Distance Approx 1½ miles
Time 2–3 hours, depending on
  indoor visits
Start point Tower Bridge
✚ K6
⊙ Tower Hill
End point Royal Festival Hall,
  South Bank
✚ G6
⊙ Waterloo
◈ Waterloo

THE SOUTH BANK: THE DESIGN MUSEUM TO WESTMINSTER BRIDGE

This walk hugs the bank of the Thames and enjoys superb views across London's core on the north bank. Begin at Tower Bridge Museum, for high-level London views. Then stroll eastwards among the old warehouses and new restaurants of Shad Thames to find Anthony Donaldson's *Waterfall* sculpture in Tower Bridge Piazza, Piers Gough's dramatic *The Circle*, the riverfront Design Museum on Butler's Wharf, and the Bramah Tea and Coffee Museum behind.

West of Tower Bridge, the path leads to H.M.S. *Belfast* and Hay's Galleria for more cafés. The London Dungeon lies behind. Outside the Cottons Centre is a pavilion where a map plots the buildings along the City view. Over London Bridge take in Southwark Cathedral, the Clink Exhibition, and a wall and rose window of the 14th-century Winchester Palace's Great Hall.

Between Southwark and Blackfriars bridges is the Shakespeare Globe Museum and Bankside Power Station (soon to be the Tate Gallery of Modern Art). The riverfront widens at the South Bank Arts Complex; beyond lies the London Aquarium. Hungerford footbridge leads to Charing Cross, Westminster Bridge to Westminster.

*Monument (1408) to
poet John Gower,
Southwark Cathedral*

16

THE TWO CITIES: CITY OF WESTMINSTER TO THE CITY OF LONDON

The heart of Westminster is still Westminster Abbey and the Houses of Parliament—there is a good view of the riverfront from the south end of Westminster Bridge.

From statue-filled Parliament Square (there is a diagram of who's who on the east side), Whitehall leads up past Downing Street—official residence of the Prime Minister—Horse Guards, and Banqueting House, to Trafalgar Square, home of the National Gallery. The National Portrait Gallery is at the end of St. Martin's Lane. Farther on, past the Coliseum, turn right through New Row into Covent Garden, a good place to stop for refreshment. On the Piazza, find the London Transport Museum and, nearby, the Theatre Museum. Down on the Strand, turn left and go through Aldwych to the Courtauld Institute Galleries on the south side.

In Fleet Street, winged dragons mark the boundary of the City of London and Westminster. Just before Chancery Lane, an alley on the right leads to Temple Church and the Inner and Middle Inns. Farther on, Johnson's Court, on the left (between nos. 166 and 167), leads to Dr. Johnson's House, while St. Bride's is on the right, tucked behind the Reuters building. St. Paul's Cathedral stands at the top of Ludgate Hill. Behind it, Watling Street leads to Bow Lane and a choice of places for lunch or dinner.

THE SIGHTS

- Westminster Bridge
- Houses of Parliament (➤ 36)
- Westminster Abbey (➤ 35)
- Parliament Square
- Whitehall
- Downing Street
- Horse Guards
- Banqueting House (➤ 37)
- National Gallery (➤ 39)
- National Portrait Gallery (➤ 38)
- Coliseum (➤ 80)
- Covent Garden (➤ 40)
- London Transport Museum (➤ 40)
- Strand
- Courtauld Institute Galleries (➤ 41)
- Fleet Street
- Temple Church (➤ 55)
- Inns of Court (➤ 60)
- Dr. Johnson's House (➤ 52)
- St. Bride's Church
- St. Paul's Cathedral (➤ 45)
- Bow Lane

INFORMATION

Distance 2–2½ miles
Time 3–6 hours, depending on museum and church visits
Start point Westminster Bridge
⊞ G6
Ⓔ Westminster
End point Bow Street
⊞ G5
Ⓔ Mansion House

Statue of 2nd Duke of Cambridge (1819–1904), by Adrian Jones, in Whitehall 17

EVENING STROLLS

London is gently lit by street-lights, neon signs and the occasional floodlight, nothing very dramatic. Look for the surviving gas lamps. Both of the following strolls end in Soho, the heart of night-time London.

INFORMATION

Royal & Aristocratic Evocations
Distance ½ mile
Time 30–40 mins
Start point Buckingham Palace
➕ F6
🚇 Green Park, St. James's Park or Victoria
End point Piccadilly Circus
➕ F5
🚇 Piccadilly Circus

The Political Path
Distance ½ mile
Time 40 mins–1 hour
Start point Westminster Bridge
➕ G6
🚇 Westminster
End point Shaftesbury Avenue
➕ F5–G5
🚇 Piccadilly Circus or Leicester Square

ROYAL & ARISTOCRATIC EVOCATIONS

Buckingham Palace's gray Portland stone has a more fairytale quality at night. In front of it glints the Queen Victoria Memorial, while St. James's Park's fountains sparkle under floodlights.

Marlborough Road leads from The Mall to Pall Mall, where gas flares may illuminate an old club's façade. The red brick of St. James's Palace glows warmly, and old gas lamps shed a gentle light on the lanes behind it and to the left up St. James's Street. Along Piccadilly, Piccadilly Circus's neon lights and Eros statue are the gateway to Shaftesbury Avenue's theaters and Soho's nightlife.

THE POLITICAL PATH

From Westminster Bridge, enjoy close-ups of the Houses of Parliament and gilded Big Ben, and distant views along the twisting Thames to St. Paul's Cathedral and the City. In Parliament Square and up Whitehall, spot who was who in the statues of London's heroes and villains.

Shaftesbury Avenue

Lutyens's fountains splash at the foot of Nelson's illuminated column in Trafalgar Square; other naval stars surround him. Up behind the National Gallery, Leicester Square's great movie theaters dwarf the crowds of visitors and the occasional street musician. Chinese Soho, perfumed by its many fine restaurants, fills the lanes north of here to Shaftesbury Avenue, the focus being Gerrard Street (pedestrians only; no cars).

ORGANIZED SIGHTSEEING

Taking a guided tour is a good way to enjoy a London panorama and gain in-depth information from a Londoner. Walking tours get deeper into London life. They have good leaders, last about two hours, are cheap, and do not need to be booked in advance. Bus tours have various pick-up points, including some hotels. See also the Thames (► 57), National Theatre (► 78–79), and Wembley Stadium (► 83).

THE BIG BUS COMPANY
Live commentary on the maroon and cream, mostly open-topped, double-decker buses; Panoramic and Stopper tours (hop-on hop-off).
✉ Waterside Way, SW17 ☎ 0181 944 7810

BUS TRIP TO MURDER
The "hit list" includes Jack the Ripper and Sweeney Todd on this evening tour (not Mon, Wed) lasting 3½ hours; reservations a must.
✉ Tragical History Tours ☎ 0181 857 1545

EVAN EVANS
Blue Badge guides for walks (for example, Jack the Ripper), river cruises, and out-of-town tours.
✉ 26 Cockspur Street, Trafalgar Square, SW1 ☎ 0181 332 2222

FRAMES RICKARDS
Blue Badge guides for general, evening, thematic (ghosts, etc.), and out-of-town tours.
✉ 11 Herbrand Street, WC1 ☎ 0171 837 3111

THE ORIGINAL LONDON SIGHTSEEING TOUR
Taped commentary (eight languages) for the tour; live commentary for 'London Plus' tours.
✉ London Coaches, Jews Road, SW18 ☎ 0181 877 1722

THE ORIGINAL LONDON WALKS
The Tuckers organize a walk for most days of the year, guided by enthusiasts and experts.
✉ P.O. Box 1708, NW6 ☎ 0171 624 3978

TAKE-A-GUIDE
Tailor-made tours by foot or car.
✉ 43 Finstock Road, W10 ☎ 0181 857 1545

Buildings and more buildings

Various societies organize tours to look at London's architecture. Architectural Dialogue (☎ 0181 341 1371) have Saturday morning and other tours led by architects and architectural historians. The Georgian Group (☎ 0171 387 1720), Victorian Society (☎ 0181 994 1019) and Twentieth Century Society (☎ 0171 250 3857) all do walks and tours, too. To see new Docklands buildings, the LDDC Visitors Centre (☎ 0171 512 1111) will suggest a guide.

Guardsman, St. James's Palace

EXCURSIONS

INFORMATION

Greenwich

Distance 4 miles from London Bridge and Tower Hill, 5 miles from Westminster Bridge

Journey time 20 mins–1 hour

🚇 Docklands Light Railway to Island Gardens, then foot tunnel

🚢 Riverboat from Westminster, Charing Cross or Tower piers

National Maritime Museum

✉ Romney Road, SE10

☎ 0181 858 4422

🕐 Daily 10–5

💷 Very expensive

Greenwich Tourist Information

✉ 46 Greenwich Church Street, Greenwich, SE10

☎ 0181 858 6376

🕐 Daily

Hampton Court

Distance Approx. 11 miles

Journey time 30 mins by train, 3–4 hours by boat

🚇 Waterloo railroad station to Hampton Court

🚢 Riverboat from Westminster Pier

Hampton Court Palace

✉ East Molesey, Surrey

☎ 0181 781 9500

🕐 Summer Tue–Sun 9:30–6; Mon 10:15–6. Winter Tue–Sun 9:30–4:30; Mon 10:15–4:30

💷 Very expensive

GREENWICH

Downstream from the City lies Greenwich. At its core is a favorite royal palace, the Queen's House, designed by Inigo Jones, which is surrounded by the Royal Naval College (formerly the Royal Naval Hospital), designed by Christopher Wren. Go early and for the whole day. There is plenty to see, plus markets and craft fairs on the weekends (▶ 74).

The National Maritime Museum, the world's largest nautical museum, fills the old Royal Hospital School and incorporates Queen's House. Up the hill is the Old Royal Observatory —the Greenwich Meridian (0° longitude), passes through here. Nearby, the hilltop terrace provides London's grandest view; behind lie the Ranger's House and the Fan Museum. Before you leave, see the Painted Hall and Chapel inside Wren's Hospital, and two special boats: the *Cutty Sark* and *Gipsy Moth IV.*

HAMPTON COURT PALACE

This is London's most impressive royal palace, well worth the journey west out of the city center. When King Henry VIII dismissed Cardinal Wolsey in 1529, he took over his already ostentatious Tudor palace and enlarged it. Successive monarchs altered and repaired both the palace and its 60 acres of Tudor and baroque gardens.

The best way to visit this huge collection of chambers, courtyards, and state apartments is to follow one of the six clearly indicated routes— perhaps Henry VIII's State Apartments or the King's Apartments built for William III, immaculately restored after a devastating fire. Outside, do not miss the Tudor gardens, the Maze, and restored Privy Garden, where there are guided historical walks each afternoon.

WINDSOR

The fairytale towers and turrets of Windsor Castle make this the ultimate queen's castle—it is indeed an official residence of the Queen and her Court. It was begun by William the Conqueror, rebuilt in stone by Henry II, and there have been embellishments ever since. Various parts are open; if the State Apartments and St. George's Chapel are closed, there is still plenty to see. Changing of the Guard at 11AM.

Outside the castle lie Windsor's pretty, medieval cobblestone lanes, Christopher Wren's Guildhall, and the delightful Theatre Royal. Beyond it, you can explore Windsor Great Park's 4,800 acres with their stunning views, or cross the Thames to Eton.

A ROBERT ADAM DOUBLE: SYON & OSTERLEY

To use public transportation and see both houses, do this trip on a Saturday.
Two magnificent country mansions and their parks lie southwest of London. At each, with meticulous attention to detail both inside and out, Robert Adam transformed a 16th-century house into an elegant neo-classical mansion.

Osterley is a rare example of a well-preserved house and 140-acre park close to London. First completed in 1575, Adam's transformation in 1760–80 was for the banker Robert Child. Thameside Syon is even more sumptuous. Its opulent furnishings were made for Hugh Smithson, 1st Duke of Northumberland, whose family still owns Syon. Don't miss the Conservatory or London Butterfly House.

Syon House

INFORMATION

Windsor
Distance 17 miles
Journey time 35–50 mins
🚉 Waterloo or Paddington

Windsor Castle
☎ 01753 868286 ext 2235
🕐 Mar–Oct daily 10–5.
Nov–Feb daily 10–4
💷 Very expensive

Windsor Tourist Information
✉ 24 High Street, Windsor
☎ 01753 852010
🕐 Mon–Sat 9:30–5, Sun 10–5

Syon & Osterley
Distance 9 miles
Journey time 1 hour to either
🚇 Osterley; then bus H28, H91
to Syon. From Syon bus
237, 267 to Kew Bridge for
Waterloo.

Syon House
✉ Brentford, Middlesex
☎ 0181 560 0881/2/3
🕐 House: Apr–Dec 15
Wed–Sun, bank holidays
11–5. Park: 10–6 or dusk.
London Butterfly House:
daily 10–3:30
💷 Expensive

Osterley Park
✉ Isleworth, Middlesex
☎ 0181 560 3918
🕐 House: Apr–Oct Wed–Sat
1–5; Sun, bank holidays
11–5. Closed Good Fri.
Park: 9–7:30 or dusk
💷 Moderate

21

WHAT'S ON

London's festivals and traditions provide free, colorful events and are often the chance to see buildings usually closed to the public. The London Tourist Board publishes a free festivals booklet; most are also in the weekly listings in the magazine *Time Out*.

JANUARY	*The sales* (most of Jan): shopping bargains
FEBRUARY	*Chinese New Year* (end of Feb): dragon dances and firecrackers in Soho
MARCH	*Chelsea Antiques Fair*: Chelsea Old Town Hall
APRIL	*Oxford and Cambridge Boat Race* (1st Saturday): Putney to Mortlake on the Thames
	London Marathon (1st Sunday)
MAY	*Chelsea Flower Show* (end of May): one of the world's best, at the Royal Hospital, Chelsea
JUNE	*Trooping the Colour* (2nd Saturday): the "Colours" (flags) are trooped before the Queen on Horseguards Parade, Whitehall
	Wimbledon (end of Jun): the world's leading tennis tournament
JULY	*Promenade Concerts—"The Proms"* (Jul and Aug): a series of classical concerts in the Albert Hall
AUGUST	*Notting Hill Carnival* (last weekend, Bank Holiday Monday): Europe's biggest
SEPTEMBER	*Election of the Lord Mayor of London* (Sep 29): the Lord Mayor and his successor-elect ride in the state coach to the Mansion House
OCTOBER	"Pearly Kings and Queens" service at St. Martin-in-the-Fields (1st Sunday)
NOVEMBER	*Bonfire Night* (Nov 5): fires and fireworks commemorate the failed "Gunpowder Plot" of 1605
	State Opening of Parliament: royal procession from Buckingham Palace to Houses of Parliament
DECEMBER	*Christmas Tree* (mid-month): the annual gift from Norway is raised in Trafalgar Square
DAILY	*The Changing of the Guard*: At St. James's Palace, Guards march to Buckingham Palace at 11:15, returning at 12:10; at Buckingham Palace, the Guard is changed at 11:30 daily Apr–Aug 7, otherwise alternate days; at Horse Guards, by the former Whitehall Palace, at 11 daily, Sun at 10; at Windsor Castle, at 11 on alternate weekdays in winter, daily in summer (never on Sun). Ceremonies are cancelled in very bad weather. ☎ 0839 123411 for current information

LONDON's
top 25 sights

The sights are shown on the maps on the inside front cover and inside back cover, numbered **1–25** *from west to east across the city*

1

ROYAL BOTANICAL GARDENS, KEW

HIGHLIGHTS

- Arriving by riverboat
- Japanese Gateway
- Gallery walks, Palm House
- Temperate House
- Springtime woods and dells
- Oak Avenue to Queen Charlotte's Cottage

INFORMATION

- ✉ Kew Road, Kew, Richmond
- ☎ 0181 332 5000
- ◷ Daily from 9:30AM. Closing time varies. Closed Dec 25, Jan 1
- 🍴 Good
- Ⓔ Kew Gardens
- 🚇 Kew Bridge
- ♿ Excellent
- 👤 Moderate
- ↔ Syon House (➤ 21)
- ❓ Guided tours 11, 2; jazz concerts 3rd week July; orchid show Feb–Mar

The Princess of Wales Conservatory

Whether the trees are shrouded in winter mists, the azaleas are bursting with blossoms or the lawns are dotted with summer picnickers reading Sunday newspapers, Kew Gardens never fail to work their magic.

Royal beginnings The 300-acre gardens, containing 44,000 different plants and many glorious greenhouses, make up the world's foremost botanical research center. But it began modestly. George III's mother, Princess Augusta, planted just 9 acres in 1759, helped by gardener William Aiton and botanist Lord Bute. Architect Sir William Chambers built the Pagoda, Orangery, Ruined Arch, and three temples. Later, George III enlarged the gardens to their present size and invited Sir Joseph Banks (head gardener 1772–1819), who had traveled with Captain Cook, to plant them with specimens from all over the world.

Victorian order When the gardens were given to the nation in 1841, Sir William Hooker became director for 24 years. He founded the Department of Economic Botany, the museums, the Herbarium, and the Library, while W. A. Nesfield laid out the lake, pond, and the four great vistas: Pagoda Vista, Broad Walk, Holly Walk, and Cedar Vista.

The greenhouses Chambers' Orangery is now the Gardens' shop and restaurant. To see plant-filled greenhouses, seek out Decimus Burton's stunning Palm House (1844–1848), his Temperate House (1860–1862, when it was the world's largest greenhouse), Waterlily House (1852), and the Princess of Wales Conservatory (1987). The newest exhibition, Evolution, is in the 1950s Australia House.

KENSINGTON PALACE & GARDENS

It gives King William III a human dimension that he suffered from asthma, a modern complaint, and so moved out of dank Whitehall Palace to a mansion in the clean air of tiny Kensington village. This royal home retains a domestic feel.

The perfect location The year he became king, 1689, William and his wife Mary bought their mansion, perfectly positioned for London socializing and country living. They brought in Sir Christopher Wren and Nicholas Hawksmoor to remodel and enlarge the house, and moved in for Christmas.

A favorite royal home Despite the small rooms, George I introduced palatial grandeur with Colen Campbell's staircase and state rooms, elegantly decorated by William Kent. Meanwhile, Queen Anne added the Orangery (the architect was Hawksmoor, the woodcarver Grinling Gibbons) and annexed a chunk of royal Hyde Park, a trick repeated by George II's wife, Queen Caroline, who created the Round Pond and Long Water to complete the 275-acre Kensington Gardens. Today, a wide variety of trees are the backdrop for sculptures by G. F. Watts, Henry Moore, and George Frampton, whose image of the fairytale Peter Pan is near the Long Water.

A very special childhood On May 24, 1819, Queen Victoria was born here. She was baptized in the splendid Cupola Room, spent her childhood in rooms overlooking the gardens (now filled with Victoria memorabilia) and, on June 20, 1837, learned here she was to be queen. After moving into Buckingham Palace, she opened to the public the State Apartments and gardens of her childhood home.

HIGHLIGHTS

- King's Grand Staircase
- Presence Chamber
- Wind dial in the King's Gallery
- King's Drawing Room
- Princess Victoria's dolls' house
- Round Pond
- Summer tea in the Orangery
- Walks
- Serpentine Gallery
- Italian Gardens

INFORMATION

- C6
- Kensington Gardens, W8
- 0171 937 9561
- Daily 10–6 (last admission 4:15). Closed Dec 24–26, Jan 1, Good Fri. Closed for major refurbishment Sep–May
- Café in palace (winter) or Orangery (summer)
- High Street Kensington or Queensway
- Few
- Expensive; family tickets
- Natural History Museum (➤ 26), Science Museum (➤ 27), Victoria & Albert Museum (➤ 28)
- Guided tour every 30 mins

3

NATURAL HISTORY MUSEUM

HIGHLIGHTS

- Cromwell Road façade
- Giant gold nugget
- Fossilized frogs
- Afghan lapis lazuli
- How the memory works
- Prehistoric animals
- Marine Invertebrate Gallery

INFORMATION

- C7
- Cromwell Road, SW7; also entrance on Exhibition Road
- 0171 938 9123
- Mon–Sat 10–5:50; Sun 11–5:50. Closed Dec 23–26
- Meals, snacks, picnic areas
- South Kensington
- Excellent
- Expensive; free after 4:30 Mon–Fri, after 5 Sat–Sun; South Kensington Museums season ticket applies
- Kensington Palace (➤ 25), Science Museum (➤ 27), V&A Museum (➤ 28)
- Regular tours; lectures, films, workshops

Top: the entrance hall
Below: the East Wing

Before you go in, look at the museum building. It looks like a striped, Romanesque cathedral and is wittily decorated with a zoo of animals to match its contents: extant animals on the west side, extinct ones on the east side.

Two museums in one The Life Galleries of this family museum were originally part of the British Museum but overflowed and were housed in Alfred Waterhouse's honey-and-blue-striped building in 1880. They tell the story of life on earth. The Earth Galleries tell the story of the earth itself, beginning with a 300-million-year-old fossil of a fern.

Dinosaurs in the Life Galleries The nave of Waterhouse's cathedral contains a plaster cast of the vast skeleton of the 150-million-year-old diplodocus (the original is in Pittsburgh, PA). In the surrounding bays are foretastes of discoveries to be made in the galleries: a pygmy chimpanzee skeleton, huge deer antlers 11,000 years old, and much more. The lively exhibition galleries, now mostly remodeled, focus on the dinosaur world, the human body, mammals, birds, the marine world, and "creepy crawlies" (the 800,000 known species of insect are added to every year), all with plenty of slides, models, and hands-on games.

The Earth Galleries These offer a fascinating exploration of our planet. The galleries are undergoing a spectacular redevelopment and are reopening in phases. The Earthquake Experience, set in a Japanese supermarket is already open, as is the Earth's Treasury.

SCIENCE MUSEUM

Even if you are no scientist, it's thrilling to understand how a plane flies, how Newton's reflecting telescope worked, or how we receive satellite television. This is science made fun.

Industry and science Opened in 1857 and once part of the Victoria & Albert Museum, this is the museum that comes closest to fulfilling Prince Albert's educational aims when he founded the South Kensington Museums after the Great Exhibition of 1851. Its full title is the National Museum of Science and Industry. Therefore, over the five floors, which contain more than 60 collections, the story of human industry, discovery and invention is recounted through various tools and products, from exquisite Georgian cabinets to a satellite launcher.

Science made fun People walk, talk, laugh and get excited by what they see here. It is fun for all ages to see how things important to us every day were invented and then developed for use. The spinning wheel, steam-engine, car and television have changed our lives. The industrial society in which we live could not do without plastic, but how is it made?

All kinds of science The 70 or so galleries arranged over six floors vary from rooms of beautiful 18th-century objects to in-depth explanations of abstract concepts. You can use the hands-on equipment in Flight Lab to learn the basic principles of flying, and then apply this knowledge in the Flight Gallery next door. The Wellcome Museum of the History of Medicine, on the topmost floors, includes an exhibit on prehistoric bone surgery and an X-ray room. The Challenge of Materials and The Science of Sport are the newest galleries.

HIGHLIGHTS

- Demonstrations
- Taking part in Launch Pad
- The hands-on basement area
- Flight Lab
- Apollo 10 module
- Puffing Billy
- Amy Johnson's aeroplane, Jason
- 18th-century watches and clocks
- Health Matters
- Historical characters explaining their achievements

INFORMATION

- ✚ C7
- ✉ Exhibition Road, SW7
- ☎ 0171 938 8000
- 🕐 Daily 10–6.
  Closed Dec 24–26
- 🍴 Café, picnic area
- 🚇 South Kensington
- ♿ Excellent, plus helplines
  ☎ 0171 938 9788
- 💷 Expensive; family and season tickets, South Kensington Museums season ticket applies; free after 4:30 daily
- ❓ Guided tours; demonstrations; historic characters; lectures; films; workshops
- ↔ Natural History Museum (► 26)

Top: Apollo 10 module in the Exploration of Space Gallery

VICTORIA & ALBERT MUSEUM

HIGHLIGHTS

- Medieval ivory carvings
- Jones porcelain collection
- Glass Gallery
- Shah Jahan's Jade Cup
- Canning Jewel
- New Raphael Gallery
- Frank Lloyd Wright Room
- Silver galleries

INFORMATION

- ✚ D7
- ✉ Cromwell Road, SW7
- ☎ 0171 938 8500
- 🕐 Mon noon–5:50; Tue–Sun 10–5:50. Closed Dec 24–26, Jan 1, Good Fri, May 1
- 🍴 Basement restaurant, café
- Ⓢ South Kensington
- ♿ Very good
- 🎟 Expensive; South Kensington Museums ticket applies
- ↔ Natural History Museum (➤ 26), Science Museum (➤ 27)
- ❓ Tours, talks, courses; concerts

Detail, façade

Part of the Victoria & Albert Museum's glory is that each room is unexpected; it may contain a French boudoir, plaster casts of classical sculptures, or exquisite contemporary glass, diverting you so happily that sometimes you will never reach your original goal.

An optimistic foundation The V&A, as it is fondly known, started as the South Kensington Museum. It was Prince Albert's vision: arts and science objects available to all people to inspire them to invent and create, with the accent on commercial design and craftsmanship. Since it opened in 1857, its collection has become so encyclopedic and international that it is today the world's largest decorative arts museum.

Bigger and bigger Its size is unmanageable: 145 galleries cover 7 miles of gallery space on six floors. Its content is even more so: barely 5 percent of the 44,000 objects in the Indian department can be on show. Larger museum objects include whole London house façades, grand rooms, and the Raphael Cartoons. Despite this, contemporary work has always been energetically bought, and continues to be: more than 2,000 works on paper are acquired annually, mostly new, and more than 60 percent of furniture entering the museum is 20th-century.

Riches and rags Not every object in the V&A is precious: there are everyday things, unique pieces, and opportunities to discover a fascination for a new subject—perhaps lace, ironwork, tiles, Indian paintings, or Japanese textiles. The best way to tackle the V&A is either to select a favorite piece and go headlong for it, or wander happily for an hour or so, feasting on any objects that catch your eye.

6

KENWOOD HOUSE & HAMPSTEAD HEATH

For many north Londoners, sunny Sunday mornings on Hampstead Heath are an essential part of life: locals walk their dogs and babies, sit reading the news-papers, enjoy the fine London views, and drop into Kenwood House to see a Rembrandt or two.

Kenwood House When in 1754 William Murray, Earl of Mansfield and George III's Chief Justice, bought his country house outside pretty Hampstead village spa, he brought in London's most fashionable architect, Robert Adam, to remodel it, and employed Humphry Repton to landscape the gardens. A later owner, Edward Guinness, Earl of Iveagh, hung the walls with Rembrandts, Gainsboroughs, Vermeers and Romneys before giving the whole package, the Iveagh Bequest, to the nation.

The people's heath When Victorian London was expanding, it was the people of Hampstead who saved their valuable, open heathland from the developers' claws. Since 1829 they have pre-served, piece by piece, a total of 825 acres of rolling woodland, open grass and spectacular views—the walled Hill Garden was added only in 1960. It is "to be kept forever…open, unenclosed and unbuilt on."

A place of many moods The heath is full of action and color when weekend kite-flyers meet on Parliament Hill. It is a place for sports, per-haps swimming or boating in Hampstead Ponds, playing hockey on East Heath, enjoying a game of tennis, or simply taking a quiet walk. There are arts celebrations, too, the best of which are the summer lakeside concerts that Londoners listen to as they picnic on the sloping lawns in front of Kenwood House.

HIGHLIGHTS

- Azaleas in the Hill Garden
- Library in Kenwood House
- Lakeside concerts
- London view from beside Kenwood House
- Oak, beech, and sweet chestnut woods
- Parliament Hill
- Crossing the Heath from Hampstead to Highgate
- Rembrandt's *Portrait of the Artist* in Kenwood House
- Carpets of spring daffodils around Kenwood

INFORMATION

- ✉ Kenwood House, Hampstead Lane, NW3
- ☎ 0181 348 1286
- 🕐 Kenwood House: Apr–Sep daily 10–6. Oct–Mar daily 10–4. Closed Dec 24–25. The Heath: daily 8AM–dusk
- 🍴 Restaurant, café
- Ⓜ Kenwood: Golders Green. The Heath: Hampstead, Belsize Park, Highgate or Kentish Town
- 🚌 Kenwood: 210, 271. Parliament Hill: 214, C2, C11, C12
- 🚉 Gospel Oak, Hampstead Heath (North London Link)
- ♿ Good
- 🆓 Free
- ❓ Guided tours for parties; indoor and outdoor concerts

7

REGENT'S PARK

HIGHLIGHTS

- Queen Mary's Gardens
- Lakeside strolls
- Lolling on deck chairs by the bandstand
- Nature Study Centre
- Boating on the lake
- Nesfield's restored Avenue Gardens
- Canal boat trip from the zoo to Little Venice
- 98 species of duck
- Picnicking on the lake's north bank
- Summer barbecues and open-air theater

INFORMATION

- ✚ E3
- ✉ Marylebone Road, NW1
- ☎ 0171 486 7905
- ◉ Whole park open by 7AM daily, until shortly before dusk (times vary monthly, posted on information boards at each gate)
- ▮▮ Restaurant, cafés
- ⊜ Baker Street, Regent's Park, Great Portland Street or Camden Town
- ♿ Very good
- ↔ London Zoo (➤ 31), Madame Tussaud's Waxworks (➤ 58), Planetarium (➤ 58)
- ❓ Information boards at each entrance include plans; boats for rent on the lake and children's boating pond; weekend bandstand music; open-air theater and musicals May–Sep

Regent's Park has all an urban explorer could wish for in a park: big open spaces, a lake to row on, spectacular gardens, ducks and swans in quantity, a variety of ideal picnic spots, theater and music, and free peeks at the elephants in the zoo.

The Prince's plan Regent's Park is the result of a remarkable coincidence of royal enlightenment, architectural theater, peaceful times, and a large tract of land becoming available. In 1811 the Prince Regent, later George IV, and his architect, John Nash, conceived and completed a Regency backbone for London stretching from St. James's Park up Regent Street and Portland Place to Regent's Park. After vast earth-moving activities, the park was given its undulating lawns, lake, garden and trees, all encircled by grand terrace backdrops and dotted with just eight of the 56 planned villas.

From the nobles to the people What was designed as a garden city for nobles is now the most elegant of London parks. It has been open to the public since 1835, when Regent's Canal was one of the busiest stretches of canal in Britain. Londoners flocked to visit the zoo, Inner Circle (later Queen Mary's) Gardens, and Avenue Gardens, which W. A. Nesfield designed in 1864. Its 487 acres easily absorb Muslims strolling from the gold-domed Central Mosque, patrons of the Open-Air Theatre, cricketers—and many others besides.

The canal at Little Venice

LONDON ZOO

When you visit the zoo be sure spend time looking at the wonderful gentle Asian elephants—first from Regent's Park, then inside the zoo—having a bath, throwing dust over their backs, eating, lazing about looking contented, and playing with their keeper.

Exotic animals for Londoners In 1826 Sir Stamford Raffles, who established Singapore Colony, founded the Zoological Society of London with Sir Humphry Davy. Four years later it opened 5 acres of its gardens to the public, and met with immediate success. The Society's own collection of exotic animals—zebras, monkeys, kangaroos and bears—was soon enlarged by the royal menagerie from Windsor Castle and the royal zoo from the Tower of London.

Extraordinary animals Over the years new arrivals have included Tommy the chimpanzee in 1835 and, in 1836, the giraffes, which set a trend for giraffe-patterned fabric. Jumbo and Alice, the African elephants, were also exceedingly popular with visitors. Meanwhile, the world's first reptile house, aquarium, and insect houses were constructed.

A modern zoo Aware of the worldwide controversy over zoos, London Zoo is maintaining its place at the forefront of animal conservation and education, housing the Institute of Zoology, which carries out research, and funding fieldwork. The Children's Zoo has a "petting paddock" and a center to teach children how to care for pets. Sloth bears, hanuman langurs and muntjac deer roam the Mappin Terraces; elsewhere you can see pygmy hippos and hear the roaring big cats.

HIGHLIGHTS

- Asian elephants
- Big cats
- Children's Zoo Pet Care Centre
- Lord Snowdon's aviaries
- Reversed lighting to see nocturnal mammals
- Feeding time for penguins
- Cavorting chimpanzees
- Polar bears
- Baby rhinos

INFORMATION

✚	E2 (for entrance)
✉	Regent's Park, NW1
☎	0171 722 3333
⏰	Apr–Oct daily 10–5:30. Nov–Mar daily 10–4. Closed Dec 25
🍴	Restaurant, cafés, & kiosks
Ⓒ	Camden Town
Ⓡ	Camden Town (Thameslink)
♿	Good
💷	Very expensive
↔	Regent's Park (➤ 30)
❓	Lectures, talks, workshops; regular animal feeding times; animal action programs daily; animal adoption schemes

Top: the elephant enclosure

31

BUCKINGHAM PALACE

INFORMATION

- ✚ F6
- ✉ The Mall, SW1
- ☎ 0171 799 2331
- 🕐 Queen's Gallery: daily 9:30–4:30 (during exhibitions).
  Royal Mews: Apr–Sep Tue–Thu 12–4; Oct–Mar Wed 12–4. Closed Ascot week and ceremonial occasions.
  State Rooms, Buckingham Palace: early Aug–early Oct daily 9:30–5:30. Last entry 4:30.
- 🚇 Victoria, St. James's Park or Green Park
- 🚉 Victoria (BR)
- ♿ Excellent
- 🖐 All very expensive
- ↔ Changing the Guard (➤ 22), St. James' Park (➤ 33)
- ❓ No photography

Of the London houses now open to visitors, the Queen's own home where she spends much of the year must be the most fascinating of all: where else can you see a living sovereign's private art, drawing rooms, and horse harnesses.

Yet another palace The British sovereigns have moved around London quite a bit over the years: from Westminster to Whitehall to Kensington and St. James's, and finally to Buckingham Palace. It was George III who, in 1762, bought the prime-site mansion, Buckingham House, as a gift for his new bride, the 17-year-old Queen Charlotte, leaving St. James's Palace to be the official royal residence.

Grand improvements When the Prince Regent finally became King George IV in 1820, he and his architect, John Nash, made extravagant changes using honey-colored Bath stone, all to be covered up by Edward Blore's façade added for Queen Victoria. Today, the 600 rooms and 40-acre garden include the State Apartments, offices for the Royal Household, a movie theater, swimming pool, and the Queen's private rooms overlooking Green Park.

Queen Elizabeth II opens her home The Queen inherited the world's finest private art collection and in 1962 built the Queen's Gallery so everyone could enjoy changing exhibitions selected from her riches. Nearby, in the Royal Mews, Nash's stables and storerooms house gleaming fairytale coaches, harnesses, and other apparel for royal ceremonies. Make sure you do not miss the Buckingham Palace Summer Opening, when visitors can wander through the grand State Rooms, resplendent with gold, pictures, porcelain, tapestries and, of course, thrones.

ST. JAMES'S PARK

Even if you drop in to St. James's Park merely to eat a sandwich and laze on a deck chair while listening to the band's music, you can usually spot a trio of palaces across the duck-filled lake and over the tips of the weeping willows.

Royal through and through St. James's Park is the oldest and most thoroughly royal of London's nine royal parks, surrounded by the Palace of Westminster, St. James's Palace, Buckingham Palace, and the remains of Whitehall Palace. Kings and their courtiers have been frolicking here since Henry VIII laid out a deer park in 1532 and built a hunting lodge that became St. James's Palace. James I began the menagerie, which included pelicans, crocodiles, and an elephant who drank a gallon of wine daily.

French order Charles II, influenced by Versailles, near Paris, redesigned the park to include a canal (where he swam), Birdcage Walk (where he kept his aviaries), and the graveled Mall, where he played pell mell, a courtly French game similar to croquet. Then George IV, helped by Nash and influenced by Humphry Repton, softened the garden's formal French lines into the English style, making this 93-acre park of blossoming shrubs and undulating, curving paths a favorite with all romantics.

Nature dominates As the park is an important migration point and breeding area for birds, two full-time ornithologists look after up to 1,000 birds from more than 45 species. Among the fig, plane and willow trees, seek out the pelicans living on Duck Island, a tradition begun when the Russian Ambassador gave some to Charles II.

HIGHLIGHTS

- Springtime daffodils
- Whitehall from the lake bridge
- Feeding the pelicans, 3PM
- Views to Buckingham Palace
- Duck Island in springtime
- The fact that it is still not enclosed

INFORMATION

✚	F6
✉	The Mall, SW1
☎	0171 930 1793
🕐	Daily dawn–midnight
🍴	Restaurant, café
Ⓔ	St. James's Park, Green Park or Westminster
🚌	Victoria
♿	Very good
💷	Free
↔	Changing the Guard (➤ 22), Buckingham Palace (➤ 32), Banqueting House (➤ 37)
?	Occasional bird talks; summer bandstand music

The Whitehall skyline seen from the park

11

TATE GALLERY

INFORMATION

- G8
- Millbank, SW1
- 0171 887 8000
- Mon–Sat 10–5:50; Sun 2–5:50. Closed Dec 24–26, Jan 1, Good Fri, May Day public holiday
- Restaurant, café
- Pimlico
- Victoria
- Very good
- Free; charge for special exhibitions
- Westminster Abbey (➤ 35)
- Guided tours; Tate Inform audioguide; lectures, workshops; films; Turner Study room

The annual Tate rehang by the director is a winter highlight: familiar pictures reappear in different places, and there are plenty of new works, both British and modern, to get to know.

Two for one The Tate, opened in 1897, is named after the sugar millionaire Henry Tate, who paid for the large national collections, displaying some of each: British art from the 16th century to around 1900; and international modern art from the Impressionists until the present day. The annual rehangs emphasize different aspects of both collections.

British art In rooms to the left of the central halls (filled with sculptures) you may well find the large icon-like portrait of Elizabeth I by Nicholas Hilliard and the Tate's earliest dated picture, John Bette's *Man in a Black Cap* (1545). There are portraits by Van Dyck, Hogarth, Gainsborough, and Reynolds, illustrations by Blake, landscapes by Constable and, in Room 9, pictures by the Pre-Raphaelites. The Turner Collection is housed in the Clore Gallery, (through Room 18), designed by James Stirling.

Modern international art Across the central halls, you will enter the modern rooms, where the more controversial works generate plenty of noisy discussion. You may find works by Monet, Matisse and Picasso, or by the more recent Mark Rothko and Jasper Johns, or by the British artists David Hockney and Peter Blake. But space is limited. This collection is to move into Giles Gilbert Scott's splendid Bankside Power Station in the year 2000, leaving this building to become the Tate Gallery for British Art in 2001.

12

WESTMINSTER ABBEY

It requires an effort to get there, but the very best time to be in the Abbey is for the 8AM service in tiny St. Faith's Chapel, and then a wander in the silent nave and cloisters before the noisy tours arrive.

The kernel of London's second city It was Edward the Confessor who in the 11th century began the rebuilding of the modest Benedictine abbey church of St. Peter which was consecrated in 1065. The first sovereign to be crowned there was William the Conqueror, on Christmas Day, 1066. Successive kings were patrons, as were the pilgrims who flocked to the Confessor's shrine. Henry III (1216–72) employed Master Henry de Reyns to re-begin the Gothic abbey that

The West Front

stands today, and Henry VII (1485–1509) built his Tudor chapel with its delicate fan-vaulting. Since William I, all sovereigns have been crowned here—even after Henry VIII broke with Rome in 1533 and made himself head of the Church of England; and all were buried here up to George II (after which Windsor became the royal burial place, ► 20–21).

Daunting riches The Abbey is massive, full of monuments, and very popular. At the west door, enjoy the view and Master Henry's achievement, then look over the Victorian Gothic choir screen into Henry V's chantry. After seeing the chapels, the royal necropolis, and Poets' Corner, leave time for the peaceful cloisters.

HIGHLIGHTS

- Portrait of Richard II
- Mid-morning choral singing
- Sir Isaac Newton memorial
- Thornhill's window
- Henry VII's Chapel
- Edward the Confessor's Chapel
- St. Faith's Chapel
- Tile floor, Chapter House
- Little Cloister and College Garden
- Weekday Sung Evensong (not Wed) at 5PM

INFORMATION

- ✚ G7
- ✉ Broad Sanctuary, SW1
- ☎ 0171 222 5152
- 🕐 Nave and cloisters: daily 8–6.
  Royal Chapels: Mon–Fri 9–4:45; Sat 9–2:45, 3:45–6. Closed Sun, Dec 24–28, Good Fri, Commonwealth Observance Day
  Abbey: open for amateur photography Wed 6PM–7:45PM (free). Closed before special services
- 🍴 Café in cloisters
- Ⓦ Westminster
- 🚌 Victoria
- ♿ Good
- 💷 Free for services; Royal Chapels expensive
- ↔ Houses of Parliament (► 36)
- ❓ Guided tours

HOUSES OF PARLIAMENT

HIGHLIGHTS

- View from Westminster Bridge
- Statue of Oliver Cromwell
- Big Ben
- Richard I's equestrian statue
- Commons or Lords debates
- Line of Route Tours
- St. Stephen's Hall
- Westminster Hall
- State Opening of Parliament
- Jewel Tower

INFORMATION

- ✚ G7
- ✉ Westminster, SW1
- ☎ 0171 219 3000.
  Commons: 0171 219 4272.
  Lords: 0171 219 3107
- Parliament: sits Mon, Tue, Thu 2:30; Wed, Fri 9:30. Closed Christmas, Easter, Whitsun and summer (late Jul–mid-Oct) recesses.
  Jewel Tower: 1 Apr–30 Sep daily 10–1, 2–6.
  1 Oct–31 Mar daily 10–1, 2–4. Closed 24–6 Dec, 1 Jan
- Westminster
- Waterloo
- Parliament: free; line up or apply for tickets from your embassy or consulate. Line of Route permits: ✉ Public Information Office, House of Commons, 1 Derby Gate. Jewel House: moderate
- ↔ Westminster Abbey (➤ 35)
- ❓ State Opening of Parliament: mid-Nov (➤ 22)

Big Ben is for many the symbol of London; they love its tower, its huge clear clockface, its thundering hour bell whose name is now given to the whole tower, and the way it glows like a reassuring beacon when illuminated at night.

Powerhouse for Crown and State William the Conqueror made Westminster his seat of rule to watch over the London merchants (he also built the Tower of London ➤ 48). It was soon the center of government for England, then Britain, then a globe-encircling empire. It was also the principal home of the monarchs until Henry VIII moved to Whitehall.

Mother of parliaments Here the foundations of Parliament were laid according to Edward I's Model Parliament of 1295: a combination of elected citizens, lords, and clergy. This developed into the House of Commons (elected Members of Parliament) and the House of Lords (unelected senior members of State and Church). Henry VIII's Reformation Parliament of 1529–36 ended Church domination of Parliament and made the Commons more powerful than the Lords.

A building fit for an empire Having survived the Catholic conspiracy to blow up Parliament (on November 5, 1605, Guy Fawkes night), almost all the buildings were destroyed by a fire in 1834. Kingdom and empire needed a new headquarters. With Charles Barry's plans and A. W. Pugin's detailed design, a masterpiece of Victorian Gothic was created. Behind the river façade decorated with statues of rulers, the Lords is on the left and the Commons on the right. If Parliament is in session, there is a flag on Victoria Tower or, at night, a light on Big Ben.

BANQUETING HOUSE

It is chilling to imagine Charles I calmly walking across the park from St. James's Palace to be beheaded outside the glorious hall built by his father. The magnificent ceiling was painted for Charles by Peter Paul Rubens.

London's most magnificent room This, all that remains of Whitehall Palace, was London's first building to be coated in smooth, white Portland stone. Designed by Inigo Jones and built between 1619 and 1622, it marked the beginning of James I's dream to replace the original sprawling Tudor palace with a 2,000-room Palladian masterpiece. In fact, it was only the banqueting hall that was built. Inside, the King hosted small parties in the crypt and presided over lavish court ceremonies upstairs.

The Rubens ceiling The stunning ceiling was commissioned by James's son, Charles I. Painted between 1634 and 1636 by Peter Paul Rubens, the leading baroque artist based in Antwerp, the panels celebrate James I, who was also James VI of Scotland. Nine allegorical paintings show the unification of Scotland and England and the joyous benefits of wise rule. Rubens was paid £3,000 and given a knighthood for the work.

The demise of Whitehall Palace This palace has brought a fair share of bad luck to its occupants. Cardinal Thomas Wolsey lived so ostentatiously that he fell from Henry VIII's favor. Henry moved in, making it his and his successors' main London royal residence. It was here that Charles I was beheaded on January 30, 1649, and William III suffered from the dank river air. A fire in 1698 wiped out the Tudor building, leaving only the stone Banqueting House.

HIGHLIGHTS

- Sculpted head of Charles I
- Weathercock put on the roof by James II
- Rubens ceiling
- Allegory of James I between Peace and Plenty
- Allegory of the birth and coronation of Charles I
- Night-time concerts
- Whitehall river terrace in Embankment Gardens
- The video and accoustiguide

INFORMATION

- G6
- Whitehall, SW1
- 0171 930 4179
- Mon–Sat 10–5. Last admission 4:30. Closed Dec 24–Jan 1, public holidays and for government functions
- Westminster, Charing Cross or Embankment
- None
- Moderate
- St. James's Park (➤ 33), National Gallery (➤ 39), Cabinet War Rooms (➤ 50)
- Occasional concerts

Inigo Jones's façade

15

NATIONAL PORTRAIT GALLERY

HIGHLIGHTS

- *Self-portrait with Barbara Hepworth*, Ben Nicholson
- Icon-like *Richard II*
- Holbein's miniature of Thomas Cromwell
- *Samuel Pepys*, John Hayl
- *Queen Victoria*, Sir George Hayter
- *The Brontë Sisters*, Branwell Brontë
- *Isambard Kingdom Brunel*, John Callcott
- *Florence Nightingale*, William White
- *Captain Scott*, Herbert Ponting
- *Sir Peter Hall*, Tom Phillips

INFORMATION

- ➕ G5
- ✉ St. Martin's Place, WC2
- ☎ 0171 306 0055
- 🕐 Mon–Sat 10–6; Sun 12–6. Closed Dec 24–26, Jan 1, Good Fri, May Day public holiday
- 🚇 Leicester Square or Charing Cross
- 🚉 Charing Cross
- ♿ Good
- 🎫 Free, except for special exhibitions
- ↔ National Gallery (➤ 39)
- ❓ Lectures; events

It is always fascinating to see what someone famous looks like and how they chose to be painted—for instance, you would never expect Francis Drake to be in red courtier's, rather than sailor's, clothes.

A British record Founded in 1856 to collect portraits of the Great and Good in British life, and so inspire others to greatness, this now huge collection is the world's most comprehensive of its kind. There are oil paintings, watercolors, caricatures, silhouettes, and photographs.

Start at the top The galleries are arranged in chronological order, starting on the top floor (which can be reached by stairs or elevator). Henry VIII and some of his wives kick off a visual Who's Who of British history that moves through inventors, merchants, engineers, explorers, and empire builders to modern politicians, always accompanied by their observers, the writers. Brunel and Jenner are here; so, too, are Clive and Hastings, Winston Churchill, and Margaret Thatcher. There is Chaucer in his floppy hat, Kipling at his desk, and A. A. Milne with Christopher Robin and Winnie-the-Pooh on his knee. Some of the lesser-known sitters merit a close look, such as the 18th-century group portrait of the remarkable and extensive Sharp Family, who formed an orchestra and played at Fulham every Sunday.

A modern record, too At first, the Victorians insisted upon entry only after death, but this rule has been broken. Among the many contemporary portraits, you may find those of the Princess Royal, Beatle Paul McCartney, soccer player Bobby Charlton, Maggie Hambling's *Stephen Fry*, and Andy Warhol's *Joan Collins*.

16

NATIONAL GALLERY

The façades may be unexciting, but here is a collection of tip-top pictures—and for free, so you can drop in for a few minutes' peace in front of Leonardo da Vinci's cartoon in the Sainsbury Wing or Rubens's ravishing Samson and Delilah.

A quality collection Founded in 1824 with just 38 pictures, the National Gallery now has about 2,000 paintings, all on show. Spread throughout William Wilkins's neo-classical building and the new Sainsbury Wing extension (opened 1991), they provide an uncramped, extremely high-quality, concise panorama of European painting from Giotto to Cézanne. Most modern and British pictures are at the Tate Gallery (► 34).

Not royal, not only British Unusually for a national painting collection, the nucleus is not royal but the collection of John Julius Angerstein, a self-made financier. From the start it was open to all, including children, free of charge, and provided a wide spectrum of British painting within a European context—aims that are still maintained. New arrivals include Dürer's *St Jerome*.

A first visit To take advantage of the rich artistic panorama, why not choose a room from each of the four chronologically arranged sections? Early paintings by Duccio di Buoninsegna, Jan van Eyck, Piero della Francesca and others fill the Sainsbury Wing. In the old building, the West Wing has 16th-century pictures, including Michelangelo's *Entombment*, while the North Wing is devoted to 17th-century artists such as Van Dyck, Rubens, Rembrandt, Velàzquez, and painters of the Dutch school. Finally, the East Wing runs from Chardin through Gainsborough to Monet, Matisse, and Picasso.

HIGHLIGHTS

- Cartoon, Leonardo da Vinci
- *Pope Julius II*, Raphael
- *The Arnolfini Wedding*, Van Eyck
- Equestrian portrait of Charles I by Van Dyck
- *The Triumph of Pan*, Poussin
- *Le Chapeau de Paille*, Rubens
- *The House of Cards*, Chardin
- *Mr. and Mrs. William Hallett*, Gainsborough
- *La Pointe de Hève*, Monet
- View from Wilkins's entrance

INFORMATION

- ✚ G6
- ✉ Trafalgar Square, WC2
- ☎ 0171 839 3321
- 🕐 Mon–Tue, Thu–Sat 10–6; Wed 10–8; Sun 2–6. Closed Dec 24–26, Jan 1, Good Fri
- 🍴 Brasserie, basement café
- Ⓔ Charing Cross or Leicester Square
- 🚆 Charing Cross
- ♿ Excellent
- 🎟 Free; charge for special exhibition
- ↔ St. James's Park (► 33), National Portrait Gallery (► 38)
- ❓ Guided tours; lectures; films; picture identification service

17

COVENT GARDEN PIAZZA

HIGHLIGHTS

- Bedford arms and motto over the Market entrances
- St. Paul's Covent Garden
- 1920s and 1930s Underground posters
- Craft stalls in Apple Market
- The Theatre Museum
- Jubilee Hall Market
- How the Underground works, London Transport Museum
- Charles H. Fox's make-up shop, Tavistock Street
- Neal Street, nearby

INFORMATION

- ✚ G5
- ✉ Covent Garden Piazza, WC2
- 🍴 Plentiful, all prices
- Ⓜ Covent Garden
- 🚆 Charing Cross
- ♿ Good
- 🎟 Free, except museums
- ↔ National Portrait Gallery (➤ 38), Courtauld Institute Galleries (➤ 41), British Museum (➤ 43), Dr. Johnson's House (➤ 52)

London Transport Museum
- ✉ 39 Wellington Street, WC2
- ☎ 0171 379 6344
- 🕐 Mon–Thu, Sat, Sun 10–6; Fri 11–6. Last admission 5:15. Closed Dec 24–26
- 🍴 Café
- ♿ Very good
- 🎟 Expensive
- ❓ Weekend guided tours; lectures; films; workshops

It is always fun to cut through the Piazza, to see perhaps a family of clowns cavorting in front of St. Paul's Church, a busker cheering on the stall-holders, and people meeting up to enjoy the City.

London's first square Charles I was against expanding beyond the City but Francis Russell, the Earl of Bedford, owned a prime piece of land just west of it. Around 1630 the Earl paid the King £2,000 for a building license and used Inigo Jones to lay out London's first residential square. An instant success, it became a distinctive London feature.

Covent Garden When society left, the vegetable market moved in, together with taverns, gambling dens, and prostitutes. Charles Fowler's Central Market (1831) brought order, as did Floral, Flower, and Jubilee Halls, making this London's central fruit and vegetable

A Punch and Judy show

market until 1974. Locals saved the area from demolition, and today the restored halls and spruced-up streets make the Piazza London's most convivial meeting place.

London Transport Museum This tells the story of the world's largest urban public transportation system, which covers more than 500,000 miles. There are buttons to push, and plenty of vehicles. Star attractions include the Underground simulator, the touch screens in six languages, actors on the vehicles—and the shop.

COURTAULD INSTITUTE GALLERIES

These sumptuously decorated galleries hung with Impressionist paintings—Renoir's La Lôge, *Manet's* Bar at the Folies-Bergère, *Cézannes, Gauguins and many more—are the perfect antidote to a gray, cloud-coated London day.*

One man's vision The industrialist Samuel Courtauld began collecting French Impressionist and Post-Impressionist paintings in 1921. Ten years later he founded the Courtauld Institute of Art. Using his own mansion designed by Robert Adam in Portman Square, he hoped that art history students would learn about paintings in the setting of fine architecture and furniture. In its new home on the Strand, the Courtauld fulfills his aim perfectly.

A palatial home A majestic, triple-arched gateway leads into Sir William Chambers's rather dull English Palladian government offices (1776–86)—no match for the work of his contemporary fellow Scot, the highly fashionable Robert Adam. Before the Embankment was built, its river façade met the Thames with great basement arches and a watergate, which you can see from Waterloo Bridge. The 11 galleries fill a string of lavishly decorated, restored rooms, once the home of the Royal Academy (► 51).

Six collections in one After Courtauld, five other collectors donated their art. Lord Lee of Fareham presented Old Masters and British works; art critic Roger Fry gave his collection; Sir Robert Witt gave his drawings (now the Witt Library, which fills the vaults); the Mark Gambier-Parry Bequest includes Italian Renaissance panels; and Count Antoine Seilern's Prince Gate Collection includes baroque painters such as Rubens, Tiepolo, and Van Dyck.

HIGHLIGHTS

- *Card Players*, Cézanne
- *Nevermore*, Gauguin
- *Peach Trees in Blossom*, van Gogh
- *Bar at the Folies-Bergère*, Manet
- *La Lôge*, Renoir
- Any of 32 Rubens paintings
- Beechey's portrait of Queen Charlotte
- *Entombment*, Master of Flemalle
- River façade viewed from Waterloo Bridge

INFORMATION

- ✚ G5
- ✉ Somerset House, Strand, WC2
- ☎ 0171 873 2526
- Mon–Sat 10–6; Sun 2–6. Last admission 5:15. Closed Dec 24–26
- 🍽 Café
- Ⓢ Temple
- 🚆 Blackfriars (BR, Thameslink), Charing Cross
- ♿ Excellent
- 👤 Moderate
- ↔ Covent Garden (► 40), Sir John Soane's Museum (► 42), Dr. Johnson's House (► 50)
- ❓ Guided tours (pre-arranged); talks by Institute students; summer concerts; prints and drawings study room

Top: detail, Gauguin's Nevermore

19

SIR JOHN SOANE'S MUSEUM

HIGHLIGHTS

- *The Rake's Progress, The Election*, Hogarth
- Sarcophagus of Seti I
- Lawrence's portrait of Soane
- Monk's Parlour
- Works by Turner, Canaletto
- Model Room

INFORMATION

- 🞢 G5
- ✉ 13 Lincoln's Inn Fields, WC2
- ☎ 0171 405 2107
- 🕐 Tue–Sat 10–5; 1st Tue of month 6–9PM. Closed Dec 24–26, Jan 1, Good Fri
- 🚇 Holborn
- 🚆 Farringdon
- 🎫 Free
- ↔ Courtauld Institute Galleries (➤ 41), British Museum (➤ 43), Dickens House (➤ 44)
- ❓ Guided tours Sat 2:30

As you move about the gloriously over-furnished rooms of Soane's two houses—he outgrew one so built a second next door—and into the calm upstairs drawing-room, his presence is so strong you feel you would not be surprised if he were there to greet you.

Soane the architect This double treasure-house in leafy Lincoln's Inn Fields, Central London's largest square, is where the neo-classical architect Sir John Soane lived. First he designed no. 12 and lived there from 1792. Then, outgrowing this, he bought no. 13 next door, rebuilt it with cunningly proportioned rooms, and lived there from 1813 until his death in 1837. Meanwhile, he also designed Holy Trinity, on Marylebone Road (1824–28), and parts of the Treasury, Whitehall. His model for his masterpiece, the (destroyed) Bank of England, is here (re-created rooms now form the bank's museum, ➤ 50). No. 14 opens as a centre for Adam Studies in 2004.

Soane the collector Soane was an avid collector. He found that every art object could inspire his work, so his rooms were a visual reference library. Hogarth's paintings unfold from the walls in layers. There are so many sculptures, paintings, and antiquities that unless you keep your eyes peeled you will miss a Watteau drawing, a Greek vase, or something even better.

The ghost of Soane Sir John's ingenious designs pervade every room, as do the stories of his passion for collecting. For example, when an Egyptian sarcophagus arrived, he gave a three-day party in its honor.

Behind the façade a labyrinth of rooms houses a bizarre collection

BRITISH MUSEUM

It's fun to choose your own seven wonders of the world in the British Museum. The bronzes from the Indian Chola dynasty and the lion-filled reliefs that once lined an Assyrian palace may well be on everyone's list, but the others will vary.

The physician founder Sir Hans Sloane, after whom Sloane Square is named, was a fashionable London physician, "interested in the whole of human knowledge" and an avid collector of everything from plants to prints. When he died in 1753 aged 92 he left his collection of more than 80,000 objects to the nation on condition that it was given a permanent home. Thus began the British Museum, opened in 1759 in a 17th-century mansion, Britain's first public museum and now its largest, covering 13½ acres.

It grew and it grew To Sloane's collection were added many others. Kings George II, III, and IV made magnificent gifts, as did other monarchs. These, with the Townley and Elgin Marbles, burst the building's seams and the architect Robert Smirke was commissioned to build a grand new museum, completed by his son, Sydney, in 1857. Even so, because the booty from expeditions and excavations poured in continuously, the Natural History collections went to South Kensington (► 26). With the departure of the British Library to north London, the museum is undergoing long-term total reorganization.

Coming to grips with the British Museum A good way to explore "that old curiosity shop in Great Russell Street" is to pick up a plan at the main entrance, see what special events are on, choose at the most three rooms to see and set off to find them. For peace and quiet, go early.

HIGHLIGHTS

- Oriental antiquities
- HSBC Money Gallery
- Rosetta Stone
- Current prints and drawings
- Islamic Art
- Mildenhall and Sutton Hoo treasures
- Elgin Marbles
- Assyrian and Egyptian rooms
- Roman Britain Gallery
- 300-foot-long King's Library

INFORMATION

- ✛ G4
- ✉ Great Russell Street, WC1
- ☎ 0171 636 1555
- 🕐 Mon–Sat 10–5; Sun 2:30–6; 1st Tue of each month 6–9PM. Closed Dec 24–26, Jan 1, Good Fri, May Day public holiday
- 🍴 Restaurant, café
- Ⓜ Holborn or Tottenham Court Road
- ♿ Very good
- 💷 Free; charge for some temporary exhibitions, tours and late opening
- ↔ Covent Garden Piazza (► 40), Percival David Foundation of Chinese Art (► 51)
- ❓ Gallery talks; guided tours; lectures (second entrance in Montague Place)

DICKENS HOUSE

HIGHLIGHTS

- Dickens's study
- Drawing Room
- Original manuscript of *Oliver Twist*
- Copy of *David Copperfield* found with the possessions of Scott of the Antarctic
- Original manuscript of *Pickwick Papers*
- Dickens's court suit
- "Phiz" illustrations
- Guided Dickens walks

INFORMATION

- ✚ H4
- ✉ 48 Doughty Street, WC1
- ☎ 0171 405 2127
- 🕐 Mon–Sat 10–5. Closed Dec 25–Jan 4 and some public holidays
- 🚇 Russell Square, Chancery Lane or King's Cross
- 🚉 King's Cross
- ♿ Few
- 💷 Moderate
- ↔ Sir John Soane's Museum (➤ 42), British Museum (➤ 43), Percival David Foundation of Chinese Art (➤ 50–51)
- ❓ Information on regular Dickens walks

Standing beside Dickens's desk and chair in the house where he and his young wife lived, it is easy to imagine him going off on his long London walks to research deprived Victorian life while he was writing Oliver Twist.

Dickens's London homes Of Charles Dickens's many London homes, this is the only survivor. He lived here between 1837 and 1839, moving from Furnival's Inn, Holborn, after he married, and leaving when his growing family forced him to go to a larger house in Devonshire Terrace. Forty-eight Doughty Street is part of a typical brick, flat-fronted, Regency terrace, but is set in a wide and handsome avenue that, like the nearby Bloomsbury Square, would have had gates at either end manned by liveried porters, and mewslanes for servants and deliveries.

Dickens at Doughty Street Here Dickens completed *Pickwick Papers*, wrote *Oliver Twist* and *Nicholas Nickleby*, and began *Barnaby Rudge*. Here, too, Dickens emerged from his pseudonym of "Boz" into the literary limelight—there are some marked-up prompt copies for his legendary literary readings. Other Dickens memorabilia includes a Fagin toby jug.

The Dickens Fellowship This society, which bought the house in 1924 and restored the drawing room to its original decor, cares for the world's most comprehensive Dickens library and many Dickens-related portraits, letters, and manuscripts. Do not miss Harlot Knight Brown's "Phiz" illustrations, and a newly acquired writing desk and three portraits. If you want to get under Dickens's skin, visit the house and then join a guided walk to explore a bit of his London.

ST. PAUL'S CATHEDRAL

To sneak into St. Paul's for afternoon evensong, and sit gazing up at the mosaics as the choir's voices soar, is to savor a moment of absolute peace and beauty.

Wren's London After the restoration of the monarchy in 1660, artistic patronage bloomed under Charles II. Then, when the Great Fire of London destroyed four-fifths of the City in 1666, Christopher Wren took center stage, being appointed King's Surveyor-General in 1669, aged just 37. The spires, towers and steeples of his 51 new churches (23 still stand) surrounded his masterpiece, St. Paul's.

The fifth St Paul's This cathedral church for the diocese of London was founded in A.D. 604 by King Ethelbert of Kent. The first four churches burned down. Wren's, built in stone and paid for with a special coal tax, was the first English cathedral built by a single architect, the only one with a dome, and the only one in the English baroque style. The funerals of Admiral Lord Nelson, the Duke of Wellington, and Sir Winston Churchill were held here; statues and memorials of Britain's famous crowd the interior and crypt.

The great climb The 530 steps to the top are worth the effort. Shallow steps rise to the Whispering Gallery for good views of Thornhill's dome frescoes and Richmond and Salviati's Victorian mosaics. The external Stone Gallery has telescopes and benches; above is the Golden Gallery. Go early or late to avoid crowds.

HIGHLIGHTS

- Sung Evensong
- Frescoes and mosaics
- Wren's Great Model in the triforium (upstairs)
- Triple-layered dome weighing 76,000 tons
- Jean Tijou's sanctuary gates
- Wellington's memorial
- *Light of the World*, Holman Hunt
- The great climb
- Wren's epitaph under the dome

INFORMATION

- ✚ J5
- ✉ St. Paul's Churchyard, EC4
- ☎ 0171 236 4128 ext 350
- 🕐 Mon–Sat 8:30–4. Galleries: Mon–Sat 9:30–4:15. Services: Mon–Sat 5; Sun 11, 3:15
- 🍴 Refectory in the crypt
- Ⓢ St. Paul's or Mansion House
- 🚉 City Thameslink or Cannon Street (BR)
- ♿ Very good
- 🅿 Moderate. Galleries: extra
- ↔ Museum of London (➤ 47), Bank of England Museum (➤ 50), Dr. Johnson's House (➤ 52), St. Margaret's Lothbury (➤ 55)
- ❓ Guided tours Mon–Sat 11, 11:30, 1:30, 2; bell-ringing practice some Tue; organ recitals most Fri lunchtimes, some Thu evenings; July summer masses; prayers every hour on the hour

23

St. Bartholomew-the-Great

HIGHLIGHTS

- Rahere's tomb
- Richard Rich's tomb
- William Bolton's window
- Medieval font
- Tudor memorial to Sir Walter Mildmay
- Ramsden church silver
- Any choral service
- The two church cats, Matins and Evensong

INFORMATION

- ✠ J4
- ✉ West Smithfield, EC1
- ☎ 0171 606 5171 (8:30–4:30)
- ⏰ Mon–Fri 8:30–5 (winter 8:30–4); Sat 10:30–1:30; Sun 2–6.
  Sun services: 9AM, 11AM (choral), 6:30PM (choral)
- 🚇 Barbican, Farringdon or St. Paul's
- 🚌 Farringdon
- ♿ Good
- 💷 Free (donation encouraged)
- ↔ St. Paul's Cathedral (➤ 45), Museum of London (➤ 47)
- ❓ Exceptional choir

A Sunday evening spent at St. Bartholomew's is truly memorable: while trucks arrive at Smithfield's meat market, you can answer the ringing bells and pass under the great stone arch into a hidden, medieval world for beautifully sung evensong.

A court jester for founder Henry I's court jester, Rahere, became an Augustinian canon. While on pilgrimage to Rome he was cured of malaria, had a vision of St. Bartholomew, and took a vow. On his return, the King gave him land to found St. Bartholomew's Hospital and Priory—London's first hospital but one of four monasteries in the area.

London's oldest church Rahere's priory church, built in 1123, is London's oldest church, the City's only 12th-century monastic church and its best surviving piece of large-scale Romanesque architecture. The remains (the nave and cloisters are gone) give an idea of the magnificence of London's dozen or so medieval monastic churches.

Entering a different world The church lies through a 13th-century stone arch topped by a Tudor gatehouse, which once led into the great priory church's west end. Today, a path runs the length of what was the ten-bay nave down to the present west door. Here is the choir, the ambulatory, and the Lady Chapel (built by Rahere), whose roofs are supported by honey-colored walls and sturdy, circular columns. The minimal decoration makes the impact all the more powerful. Two tombs sit uneasily together here: those of the founder, Rahere (died 1143, tomb 1404), and of the destroyer, Richard Rich, who bought the building from Henry VIII after the dissolution of the monasteries.

MUSEUM OF LONDON

A visit here is easily the best way to cruise through London's 2,000 years of history, pausing to see a Roman shoe, the Lord Mayor's State Coach, or an old shop counter; and it is even built on top of the West Gate of London's Roman fort.

A museum for London This is the world's largest and most comprehensive city museum, opened in 1975 in a building by Powell and Moya. The collection combines the old Guildhall Museum's City antiquities with the London Museum's costumes and other culturally related objects. Plenty of building work and redevelopment in the City of London in the 1980s, allied with increased awareness about conservation, has ensured a steady flow of archaeological finds into the collection.

A museum about London The story of London is long and can be confusing. The building is, appropriately, in the barbican of the Roman fort, and the rooms are laid out chronologically to keep the story clear. Starting with prehistoric and Roman times (do not miss the peep-hole window down to 2nd-century barbican remains), the rooms work through the medieval, Tudor and Stuart period. A highlight here is the re-enactment of the Great Fire of London in 1666. The Georgian, Victorian, and 20th-century rooms mix low life with high, ranging from Newgate Gaol and the Blitz Experience to Spitalfields silks, and high-fashion stores, and ending with the London Now Gallery

A museum about Londoners People make a city, so in every room it is Londoners who are really telling the story, whether it is through their Roman storage jars, their Tudor leather clothes, or their Suffragette posters.

HIGHLIGHTS

- Neolithic bowl
- Roman letter addressed "Londinio"
- Roman wall remnants
- Viking grave
- Fragments from the Eleanor Cross
- Tudor jewelry
- Model of Tudor London
- Pepys's chess set
- 15th-century paneled room
- London Now Gallery

INFORMATION

- ✚ J4
- ✉ 150 London Wall, EC2
- ☎ 0171 600 3699
- 🕐 Tue–Sat 10–5:50; Sun 12–5:50. Closed Dec 24–26, Jan 1
- 🍴 Restaurant, café
- 🚇 Barbican, Moorgate or St. Paul's
- 🚉 Moorgate, Farringdon, Liverpool Street or City Thameslink
- ♿ Excellent
- 🎟 Moderate; all tickets valid for three months
- ↔ St. Paul's Cathedral (➤ 45), St. Bartholomew-the-Great (➤ 46), Barbican (➤ 78–79)
- ❓ Lectures; gallery talks and performances; seminars, workshops; "Made in London" film series

Mural depicting a scene from the Great Fire   47

H.M. THE TOWER OF LONDON

HIGHLIGHTS

- Medieval Palace
- Raleigh's room
- Imperial State Crown
- Tower ravens
- Grand Punch Bowl, 1829
- St. John's Chapel

INFORMATION

- ✚ K5
- ☎ 0171 709 0765
- ◷ Mar–Oct Mon–Sat 9–6; Sun 10–6. Nov–Feb Sun–Mon 10–5; Tue–Sat 9–5. Closed Dec 24–26, Jan 1
- 🍴 Cafés
- Ⓔ Tower Hill
- 🚉 Fenchurch Street, Cannon Street or London Bridge
- ♿ Excellent for Jewel House
- 💷 Very expensive
- ↔ Design Museum (➤ 50), H.M.S. *Belfast* (➤ 57), Tower Bridge Museum (➤ 57)
- ❓ Tours every 30 mins

A "Beefeater"

The medieval palace, where Edward I lived at the end of the 13th century, brings the Tower alive as the royal palace and place of pageantry it was; for some, it's more interesting than the Crown Jewels.

Medieval fortress The Tower of London is Britain's best medieval fortress. William the Conqueror (1066–87) began it as a show of brute force, and Edward I (1272–1307) completed it. William's Caen stone White Tower, built within old Roman walls, was an excellent defense: it was 90 feet high, with walls 15 feet thick, and space for soldiers, servants and nobles. Henry III began the Inner Wall, the moat, his own watergate—and the royal zoo. Edward I completed the Inner Wall, built the Outer Wall, several towers, and Traitor's Gate, and moved the mint and Crown Jewels here from Westminster.

Scenes of splendor and horror Stephen (1135–54) was the first king to live here, James I (1603–25) was the last. From here Edward I went into procession to his coronation and Henry VIII paraded through the City bedecked in cloth of gold. Here the Barons seized the Tower to force King John to put his seal to the Magna Carta in 1215; and here two princes were murdered while their uncle was being crowned Richard III. Since 1485 it has been guarded by Yeoman Warders or "Beefeaters".

Seven centuries of history The Tower has been palace, fortress, state prison and execution site. There is much to see. Come early and see the Crown Jewels and the Crowns and Diamonds Exhibition, then take a break along the Wharf.

LONDON's
best

49

MUSEUMS & GALLERIES

Dulwich Picture Gallery

Dulwich Picture Gallery's magnificent core collection of 400 paintings was assembled for the King of Poland's projected national gallery. When the king abdicated, the collection was offered unsuccessfully to Britain for the same purpose. The art dealer who put it together, Noel Desenfans, gave it to Sir Francis Bourgeois, who donated it to Dulwich College. Housed in a building designed by Sir John Soane, and opened in 1814, it was England's first public art gallery.

The Edwardian Room, in the Geffrye Museum

BANK OF ENGLAND MUSEUM
See how Britain's monetary system and banking ideas have grown since 1694.
➕ J5 ✉ Bartholomew Lane, EC3 ☎ 0171 601 5545 🕐 Mon–Fri 10–5. Closed Dec 25–26, public holidays 🚇 Bank 🎫 Free

CABINET WAR ROOMS
The underground headquarters for Sir Winston Churchill's War Cabinet during World War II.
➕ G6 ✉ Clive Steps, King Charles Street, SW1 ☎ 0171 930 6961 🕐 Daily 10–5:15. Closed Dec 24–26 🚇 St James's Park or Westminster 🎫 Moderate

DESIGN MUSEUM
Founded by design guru Sir Terence Conran to stimulate design awareness; good shop.
➕ L6 ✉ Butler's Wharf, Shad Thames, SE1 ☎ 0171 403 6933 🕐 Mon–Fri 11:30–6; Sat, Sun 12–6. Closed Dec 25–26, Jan 1 🍴 Café 🚇 Tower Hill or London Bridge 🚉 London Bridge 🎫 Expensive

DULWICH PICTURE GALLERY
European art in a beautiful setting. See panel.
➕ Off map at K10 ✉ College Road, SE21 ☎ 0181 693 5254 🕐 Tue–Fri 10–5; Sat 11–5; Sun 2–5. Closed Dec 25–26, public holidays 🍴 Summer tea tent 🚉 North or West Dulwich 🎫 Moderate; free on Fri

GEFFRYE MUSEUM
Almshouses furnished in period style, 1550–1950.
➕ K3 ✉ Kingsland Road, E2 ☎ 0171 739 9893 🕐 Tue–Sat 10–5; Sun and public

holiday Mon 2–5PM. Closed Dec 25–26, Jan 1, Good Fri 🍴 Café
🚇 Old Street, bus 22A, 243; Liverpool Street, bus 22B, 149 🎫 Free

HAYWARD GALLERY
Major venue for art exhibitions.
➕ H6 ✉ South Bank, SE1 ☎ 0171 928 3144 🕐 Daily 10–6;
during exhibitions Tue–Wed 10–8 🍴 café 🚇 Waterloo
🚉 Waterloo 🎫 Moderate

HOUSE MUSEUMS ➤ 52

IMPERIAL WAR MUSEUM
Focuses on the social impact of 20th-century warfare through film, painting, and sound archives.
➕ H7 ✉ Lambeth Road, SE1 ☎ 0171 416 5000 🕐 Daily
10–6. Closed Dec 25–26, Jan 1 🍴 Restaurant, café
🚇 Lambeth North, Elephant & Castle or Waterloo 🚉 Waterloo
🎫 Expensive

LONDON AQUARIUM
An aquatic spectacular: follow the story of a
stream, an ocean, a coral reef, and more.
➕ G6 ✉ County Hall, Riverside Building, Westminster Bridge
Road, SE1 ☎ 0171 967 8000 🕐 Jun–Aug, public holidays daily
9:30– 7:30. Otherwise Mon–Fri 10–6; Sat–Sun 9:30–6. Last admission 1 hour before closing. Closed Dec 25 🍴 Café 🚇 Westminster
🎫 Expensive

*The Pacific Tank at the
London Aquarium*

MUSEUM OF THE MOVING IMAGE
The story of film, TV, and animation. Plenty of
participation.
➕ H6 ✉ South Bank, SE1 ☎ 0171 928 3535 🕐 Daily 10–6.
Last admission 5. Closed Dec 25–26 🚇 Embankment or Waterloo
🚉 Waterloo 🎫 Expensive

PERCIVAL DAVID FOUNDATION OF CHINESE ART
Sublime Chinese ceramics.
➕ G4 ✉ 53 Gordon Square, WC1 ☎ 0171 387 3909
🕐 Mon–Fri 10:30–5. Closed Christmas, New Year, Easter, public
holidays 🚇 Russell Square 🎫 Free

ROYAL ACADEMY
Major art shows, plus the annual Summer Exhibition.
➕ F6 ✉ Burlington House, Piccadilly, W1 ☎ 0171 439 7438
🕐 Daily 10–6. Closed Dec 25–26, Good Fri 🍴 Restaurant, café
🚇 Green Park or Piccadilly 🎫 Expensive

TOWER BRIDGE MUSEUM ➤ 57

WALLACE COLLECTION
Art collection in 18th-century townhouse. See panel.
➕ E5 ✉ Hertford House, Manchester Square, W1
☎ 0171 935 0687 🕐 Mon–Sat 10–5; Sun 2–5. Closed Dec 25–26,
Jan 1, May Day public holiday 🚇 Bond Street 🎫 Free

WHITECHAPEL ART GALLERY
The hub of vibrant East End art activities.
➕ L5 ✉ 80 Whitechapel High Street, E1 ☎ 0171 522 7888
🕐 Tue–Sun 11–5 (Wed 11–8) 🍴 Café 🚇 Aldgate East 🎫 Free

The Wallace Collection

The Wallace Collection is the
product of five generations of
discerning art collectors. The
1st Marquess of Hertford bought
Ramsays and Canalettos; the
2nd acquired Gainsborough's
Mrs. Robinson; the 3rd preferred
Sèvres and Dutch 17th-century
pictures; and the 4th, in Paris
during the Revolution, snapped
up quality French art. His
illegitimate son, Sir Richard
Wallace, added his own Italian
majolica, Renaissance armor,
bronzes, and gold.

51

HOUSE MUSEUMS

Dr. Johnson's House

See Top 25 Sights for
BANQUETING HOUSE (➤ 37)
BUCKINGHAM PALACE (➤ 32)
DICKENS HOUSE (➤ 44)
KENSINGTON PALACE (➤ 25)
KENWOOD HOUSE (➤ 29)
KEW PALACE (➤ 24)
SIR JOHN SOANE'S MUSEUM (➤ 42)

APSLEY HOUSE (WELLINGTON MUSEUM)
Splendid mansion built for Arthur Wellesley, the Duke of Wellington (1759–1852).
➕ E6 ✉ Hyde Park Corner, SW1 ☎ 0171 499 5676 🕔 Tue–Sun 11–5. Closed Dec 25–26, Jan 1, May public holiday 🚇 Hyde Park Corner 💷 Expensive

CARLYLE'S HOUSE
Thomas Carlyle, Scottish philosopher and historian, lived here from 1834 until his death in 1881.
➕ D8 ✉ 24 Cheyne Row, SW3 ☎ 0171 352 7087 🕔 Apr–Oct Wed–Sun and public holiday Mon 11–5. Last admission 4:30. Closed Nov–Mar 🚇 Sloane Square 💷 Moderate

CHISWICK HOUSE
Lord Burlington's exquisite country villa (1725–29).
➕ Off map at A8 ✉ Burlington Lane, W4 ☎ 0181 995 0508 🕔 Apr–Sep daily 10–1, 2–6. Oct–Mar Wed–Sun 10–1, 2–4. Closed Dec 24–26 🍴 Café 🚇 Turnham Green 🚋 Chiswick 💷 Moderate

DR. JOHNSON'S HOUSE
Dr. Samuel Johnson lived here between 1749 and 1759 while compiling his dictionary.
➕ H5 ✉ 17 Gough Square EC4 ☎ 0171 353 3745 🕔 May–Sep Mon–Sat 11–5:30. Oct–Apr Mon–Sat 11–5. Closed Dec 25–26, Jan 1 🚇 Chancery Lane or Blackfriars 🚋 Blackfriars 💷 Moderate

HAM HOUSE
Thameside mansion (1610), refurbished in baroque style; 17th-century garden.
➕ Off map at A10 ✉ Ham, Richmond, Surrey ☎ 0181 940 1950 🕔 House: Apr–Oct Mon–Wed 1–5; Sat–Sun 12–5. Closed Nov–Mar. Gardens: Sat–Thu 10:30–6 (or dusk). Closed Dec 24–26, Jan 1 🍴 Restaurant 🚇 Richmond, then bus 371 💷 Expensive

Leighton House

Lord Leighton made his reputation when Queen Victoria bought one of his paintings. George Aitchison then designed his home-cum-studio (1861–66). The fashionable painter and esthete gave the rooms rich red walls edged with ebonized wood. Their centerpiece is the Arab Hall, one of London's most exotic rooms, lined with Persian and Saracenic blue and green tiles collected by Leighton during his travels.

LEIGHTON HOUSE
See panel.
➕ B7 ✉ 12 Holland Park Road, W14 ☎ 0171 602 3316 🕔 Mon–Sat 11–5:30. Closed Dec 24–26, Jan 1, Easter, public holidays 🚇 High Street Kensington 💷 Free

SUTTON HOUSE ➤ 60

WALLACE COLLECTION ➤ 51

STATUES & MONUMENTS

BURGHERS OF CALAIS
Auguste Rodin's muscular bronze citizens (1915).
🚇 G7 ✉ Victoria Tower Gardens, SW1 🚇 Westminster

CHARLES I
This superb equestrian statue of Charles I was made by Hubert Le Sueur in 1633.
🚇 G6 ✉ South side of Trafalgar Square 🚇 Charing Cross
🚉 Charing Cross

DUKE OF WELLINGTON
The only London hero to have three equestrian statues: the others are in St. Paul's Cathedral and outside the Duke's home, Apsley House (► 52).
🚇 J5 ✉ Opposite the Bank of England, EC2 🚇 Bank

EROS
Alfred Gilbert's memorial (1893) to the philanthropic 7th Earl of Shaftesbury (1801–85) actually portrays the Angel of Christian Charity, not Eros.
🚇 F5 ✉ Piccadilly Circus, W1 🚇 Piccadilly Circus

MONUMENT
Wren's 202-foot Doric column commemorates the Great Fire (1666). Worth climbing the 311 steps for the view.
🚇 K5 ✉ Monument Street, EC3 🚇 Monument

NELSON'S COLUMN
Horatio, Viscount Nelson (1758–1805) went up on to his 172-foot column in 1843; the hero died as he defeated the French and Spanish at Trafalgar.
🚇 G6 ✉ Trafalgar Square 🚇 Charing Cross 🚉 Charing Cross

OLIVER CROMWELL
King-like Cromwell, Lord Protector of England from 1653 to 1658, looks across Parliament Square.
🚇 G7 ✉ Houses of Parliament 🚇 Westminster

PETER PAN
George Frampton's statue (1912) of J. M. Barrie's creation, the boy who never grew up.
🚇 C6 ✉ Long Water, Kensington Gardens 🚇 Lancaster Gate

QUEEN ALEXANDRA
This art nouveau bronze designed by Alfred Gilbert, a memorial to Edward VII's Danish-born wife, was commissioned by her daughter-in-law, Queen Mary.
🚇 F6 ✉ Marlborough Road, SW1 🚇 Green Park

SIR ARTHUR SULLIVAN
William Goscombe John's bronze of the operetta composer Sir Arthur Sullivan (1842–1900).
🚇 G5 ✉ Embankment Gardens 🚇 Embankment

The Broadgate Centre

Part of the rampant redevelopment of the City in the 1980s, Broadgate (► 54) was exceptional for its commissioning of public art. *Fulcrum* by Richard Serra—vast steel sheets tentatively resting against each other—mark the Broadgate square entrance. Beyond are Barry Flanagan's *Leaping Hare on Crescent and Bell* and George Segal's *Rush Hour*. In the center of Broadgate is the circular Arena, which becomes an outdoor ice rink in winter. Around its edge are chic restaurants, wine bars, and some shops.

Peter Pan, in Kensington Gardens

53

MODERN BUILDINGS

Designer store interiors

Sophisticated consumers have inspired retailers to create a stylish ambience in which to shop. Eva Jiricna has remodeled the Joseph shops (✉ 16 and 26 Sloane Street, SW1 and others) with her signature staircase, cable balustrades, and polished white plaster walls. Stanton Williams revamped Issey Miyake (✉ 270 Brompton Road, SW3), Branson Coates did Katharine Hamnett (✉ 20 Sloane Square, SW1) and Jigsaw (✉ 9 Argyll Street, W1 and others), and Wickham & Associates made Fifth Floor Harvey Nichols (➤ 71) a foodie's wonderland.

Broadgate

BROADGATE
This 29-acre mall and office development (1984–91) is distinguished by its impressive façades, large atria, open-air ice rink (Oct–Apr), and lunchtime events (summer). The architects were Arup Associates, Skidmore, Owings & Merrill, Inc. (Also ➤ 53 panel.)
➕ K4   ✉ EC2   ☎ 0171 505 4000   🕐 24 hours   🍴 Many   🚇 Liverpool Street

CANARY WHARF TOWER
César Pelli's soaring, blue-topped tower, the first to be clad in stainless steel, dominates Canary Wharf; Pelli describes it as "a square prism with pyramidal top in the traditional form of the obelisk."
✉ 1 Canada Square, Canary Wharf, Isle of Dogs, E14   🕐 Public spaces are open, not buildings   🚇 Canary Wharf

EMBANKMENT PLACE: CHARING CROSS
Using the air rights above Charing Cross Station, Terry Farrell & Company created 355,000 square yards of office space between 1987 and 1990, suspended on bowstring arches.
➕ G6   ✉ Villiers Street, WC2   🕐 Public space   🍴 Many   🚇 Charing Cross

FINANCIAL TIMES PRINT WORKS
Built in a year in 1988, Nicholas Grimshaw and Partners' building is designed around two vast printing presses; printing can be watched through one huge window.
✉ 240 East India Dock Road, E14   🕐 No public access, but visit 9:30–2:30 and watch the presses running   🚇 All Saints

SACKLER GALLERIES
At Foster Associates' dazzling, airy rooftop galleries, light-sensitive louvers automatically control sunlight through fretted-glass windows.
➕ F6   ✉ Royal Academy of Arts (➤ 51)

WATERLOO INTERNATIONAL STATION
Designed by Nicholas Grimshaw and Partners, this is one of the world's longest railroad stations, built to handle up to 15 million passengers a year; the viaduct structure for five new tracks is spanned by a dramatic, glazed bowstring arch.
➕ H6   ✉ SE1   🕐 Public space   🍴 Many   🚇 Waterloo

WEST ZENDERS
The latest glass curtain-wall technology made possible the building of Rick Mather's ultimate see-and-be-seen restaurant in 1991, where all three dining floors are visible from the street.
➕ G5   ✉ 4a Upper St. Martin's Lane, WC2   ☎ 0171 497 0376   🕐 Lunch, dinner   🍴 Bar, restaurant   🚇 Leicester Square

CHURCHES & CATHEDRALS

ALL-HALLOWS-BY-THE-TOWER
Begun about 1000, the church contains a Roman pavement and a carving by Grinling Gibbons.
➕ K5 ✉ Byward Street, EC3 ☎ 0171 481 2928 🕓 Church: Mon–Fri 9–6; Sat- Sun 10–5. Undercroft Museum: daily 10–4:30 🚇 Tower Hill 🎧 Charge for audiotour

CHELSEA OLD CHURCH
Begun in 1157 but much rebuilt. One of the best series of monuments in a London parish church.
➕ D8 ✉ Old Church Street, SW3 ☎ 0171 352 7978 🕓 Mon–Sat 10–1, 2–5; Sun 1:30–6 🚇 Sloane Square 🎫 Free

ORATORY OF ST. PHILIP NERI
Also known as the Brompton or London Oratory; fine baroque interior.
➕ D7 ✉ Brompton Road, SW7 ☎ 0171 589 4811 🕓 Daily 6:30AM–8PM 🚇 South Kensington 🎫 Free

ST. ETHELDREDA'S CHAPEL
This Gothic chapel survives from the Bishops of Ely's medieval townhouse.
➕ H4 ✉ Ely Place, EC1 ☎ 0171 405 1061 🕓 Daily 7:30–7 🚇 Chancery Lane or Farringdon 🚉 Farringdon 🎫 Donation encouraged

ST JAMES'S, PICCADILLY
Wren's chic church (1682–1684) for local aristocracy has a sumptuous interior.
➕ F6 ✉ Piccadilly, SW1 ☎ 0171 734 4511 🕓 Daily 8:30–7 🍴 Café 🚇 Piccadilly Circus 🎫 Donation encouraged

ST. MARGARET, LOTHBURY
Wren's church (1686–1690) retains its huge carved screen with soaring eagle and carved pulpit tester.
➕ J5 ✉ Lothbury, EC2 ☎ 0171 606 8330 🕓 Mon–Fri 8–5 🚇 Bank 🎫 Donation encouraged

TEMPLE CHURCH
Begun about 1160, this private chapel has a circular plan inspired by Jerusalem's Dome of the Rock. Effigies honor the Knights Templar, protectors of pilgrims to the Holy Land.
➕ H5 ✉ Inner Temple, EC4 ☎ 0171 353 1736 🕓 Wed–Fri 10–4; Sat 11–4; Sun 12:30–2:45. Closed for private functions 🚇 Temple 🎫 Free

Chapels Royal
London's five Chapels Royal are at St. James's Palace, Queen's Chapel, the Tower (St. Peter ad Vincula and St. John's) and Hampton Court Palace. The best services to attend are at St. Peter ad Vincula, St. James's Palace and Hampton Court, as each retains a lavish, courtly atmosphere and has a superb choir.

The Oratory of St. Philip Neri (Brompton Oratory), by Herbert Gribble (1876)

GREEN SPACES

London is almost 11 percent parkland and has 67 square miles of green space, including the nine royal parks, former royal hunting grounds.

See Top 25 Sights for
HAMPSTEAD HEATH (▶ 29)
KENSINGTON GARDENS (▶ 25)
REGENT'S PARK (▶ 30)
ROYAL BOTANICAL GARDENS, KEW (▶ 24)
ST. JAMES'S PARK (▶ 33)

BUNHILL FIELDS
Leafy City oasis, where trees shade the tombs of Blake and Defoe.
➕ J4 ✉ City Road, EC1 ☎ 0181 472 3584 🕐 Mon–Fri 7:30–7 (winter 7:30–4); Sat–Sun 9:30–4 🚇 Old Street 🎟 Free

Riders in Rotten Row, Hyde Park

GREEN PARK
Peaceful royal park.
➕ F6 ✉ SW1 ☎ 0171 930 1793 🕐 Daily dawn–dusk 🚇 Green Park or Hyde Park Corner 🎟 Free

GREENWICH ▶ 20

HOLLAND PARK
Woodland and open lawns fill 54 acres around Holland House.
➕ A6 ✉ W11 ☎ 0171 602 2226 🕐 Daily 8–dusk 🍴 Restaurant, café 🚇 Holland Park 🎟 Free

Royal parks

The nine royal parks, mostly former hunting grounds, are Londoners' substitute backyards. They also act as the city's green lungs. Many are also important bird sanctuaries. Their open spaces, woods, meadows, ponds, and wide variety of mature trees have been the setting for events ranging from the Great Exhibition of 1851 to riotous demonstrations. Today, they are places to meet, picnic, play games and, in summer, enjoy a concert or a play.

HOLY TRINITY, BROMPTON
A large, tree-shaded, airy churchyard, useful between South Kensington Museum visits.
➕ D7 ✉ Brompton Road, SW7 🕐 24 hours 🚇 South Kensington 🎟 Free

HYDE PARK
One of London's largest open spaces, tamed by Queen Caroline's gardener.
➕ D6 ✉ W2 ☎ 0171 298 2100 🕐 Daily 5–midnight 🍴 Restaurant, café 🚇 Marble Arch, Lancaster Gate, Knightsbridge or Hyde Park Corner 🎟 Free

PRIMROSE HILL
One of London's best panoramas.
➕ D2 ✉ NW3 ☎ 0171 486 7905 🕐 24 hours 🚇 St. John's Wood or Camden Town 🎟 Free

RUSSELL SQUARE
Lawns, trees and café near the British Museum.
➕ G4 ✉ WC1 🕐 Daily 7–dusk 🍴 Café 🚇 Russell Square 🎟 Free

THAMES SIGHTS

London grew up around the Thames. As the port expanded, so did London's wealth and power. The Thames was its main thoroughfare, used by all.

See Top 25 Sights for
COURTAULD INSTITUTE GALLERIES (➤ 41)
H.M. THE TOWER OF LONDON (➤ 48)
HOUSES OF PARLIAMENT (➤ 36)
ROYAL BOTANICAL GARDENS (➤ 24)
TATE GALLERY (➤ 34)

BAZALGETTE'S EMBANKMENT ➤ 12

CLEOPATRA'S NEEDLE
The 86-foot-tall pink-granite obelisk made in 1450 BC records the triumphs of Rameses the Great.
➕ G6 ✉ Victoria Embankment, WC2 🚇 Embankment or Charing Cross 🎫 Free

DOCKLANDS
Waterparks, the high-level Docklands Light Railway, Island Gardens and ambitious buildings.
✉ LDDC Visitors Centre, 3 Limeharbour, E14 ☎ 0171 512 1111
🕐 Mon–Fri 8:30–6; Sat–Sun 9:30–5. Closed Dec 25–26
🚆 Crossharbour DLR 🎫 Free

DRAGONS ON THE EMBANKMENT
The silver cast-iron dragons (1849) mark the border between the cities of London and Westminster.
➕ H5 ✉ Victoria Embankment, WC2 🚇 Temple

SMUGGLERS' PUBS, WAPPING
The Town of Ramsgate and Prospect of Whitby are atmospheric one-time smugglers' pubs.
➕ L6 ✉ Wapping, E1 🔔 Town of Ramsgate
0171 488 2685; Prospect of Whitby 0171 481 1095
🕐 Mon–Fri 11:30–3, 5:30–1; Sat 11:30–11PM; Sun 12–10:30 🍴 Bar food 🚇 Wapping
🚆 Limehouse DLR

TOWER BRIDGE MUSEUM
Opened in 1894; fine views from the museum and catwalk between the towers; engine rooms at the south bank end.
➕ K6 ✉ Tower Bridge, SE1 ☎ 0171 407 0922
🕐 Apr–Oct daily 10–6:30. Nov–Mar daily 9:30–6.
Last admission 75 mins before closing. Closed Dec 25–26, Jan 1, Good Fri 🚇 Tower Hill ⛴ Riverboat to Tower Pier 🎫 Expensive

WATERLOO BRIDGE
Gilbert Scott's cantilevered concrete; superb views.
➕ H6 ✉ WC2 🚇 Waterloo ⛴ Waterloo to Charing Cross Pier

Riverboats
On a sunny day take the Underground to Westminster and catch a riverboat up or down the Thames for the morning. Trips downstream pass Westminster, the City, and Docklands, stopping at Charing Cross, Tower, and Greenwich piers. A longer trip upstream meanders past London's villages, stopping at Putney Bridge, Kew, Richmond, and Hampton Court piers.

The Prospect of Whitby, an old riverside smugglers' pub in Wapping

FAMILY FAVORITES

Backstage tours

Going behind the scenes is great fun. In London, there are some excellent backstage tours. See how the scenery, props, and costumes are made at the National Theatre (➤ 79), or explore backstage at the Royal Shakespeare Company's Barbican and Pit theaters (➤ 79). Or you can have the crowds cheer for you when you visit Wembley Stadium (➤ 83).

BETHNAL GREEN MUSEUM OF CHILDHOOD

This outpost of the Victoria & Albert Museum (➤ 28) is an enormous train shed packed with Noah's arks, dolls, toy soldiers, puppets, and even a model circus.

➕ M3 ✉ Cambridge Heath Road, E2 ☎ 0181 983 5200 Mon–Thu, Sat 10–5:50; Sun 2:30–5:50. Closed Dec 25–26 🍴 Café Ⓔ Bethnal Green 🚆 Bethnal Green 🎟 Free

HAMLEYS

Central London's biggest toy shop, a seven-floor wonderland.

➕ F5 ✉ 188 Regent Street, W1 ☎ 0171 734 3161 Ⓔ Mon–Wed, Fri 10–7; Thu 10–8; Sat 10–7; Sun 12–6. Closed Dec 25 and occasional Sun 🍴 Café Ⓔ Oxford Circus 🎟 Free

H.M.S. BELFAST

You will need to put aside two hours to clamber up, down, and around this 1938 war cruiser, visiting the cabins, gun turrets, bridge, and boiler-room.

➕ K6 ✉ Morgan's Lane, Tooley Street, SE1 ☎ 0171 407 6434 Ⓔ Mar–Oct daily 10–6. Nov–Feb daily 10–5. Closed Dec 24–26 🍴 Café Ⓔ London Bridge 🚆 London Bridge 🎟 Moderate; family ticket

LONDON DUNGEON

Find eerie torture chambers and Jack the Ripper, and be sentenced to death.

➕ K6 ✉ 28–34 Tooley Street, SE1 ☎ 0171 403 0606 Ⓔ Daily 10–5:30. Last admission 4:30. Closed Dec 25 🍴 Restaurant, café Ⓔ London Bridge 🚆 London Bridge 🎟 Very expensive

MADAME TUSSAUD'S AND THE LONDON PLANETARIUM

Madame Tussaud learned the art of waxworks from her uncle; see how many people you can identify, from Shakespeare to Madonna, and do not miss the Spirit of London ride.

The Planetarium has good star shows and an interactive exhibition area.

➕ E4 ✉ Marylebone Road, W1 ☎ 0171 935 6861 Ⓔ Sat–Sun 9:30–5:30; Mon–Fri 10–5:30 (holiday periods from 9:30). Planetarium closed schoolday mornings. Both closed Dec 25 🍴 Restaurant, café Ⓔ Baker Street 🎟 Very expensive; family ticket; Tussaud's/Planetarium combined ticket. Discount tickets for Rock Circus (see opposite) available here

OPEN-TOPPED BUS: LONDON PLUS

Cruise about town on an open-topped double-decker

Model theaters in Pollock Toy Musuem

bus marked "Hop-on hop-off"; tickets and route maps available on board.

🚇 Moves around Central London ✉ Pick-up points include Victoria Street, Haymarket, Marble Arch, with stops in between ☎ 0181 877 1722 🕐 10–4 🚇 See above 💷 Very expensive, valid all day (or a day and a half if bought after lunch)

PEPSI TROCADERO

Segaworld, Imaginator, Virtual Glider, Funland Bumper Cars, Lazerbowl, Virtuality, the Pepsi IMAX 3D cinema and Drop of Fear provide a giant dream world of rides, adventure and interactive experiences spread over six huge floors.

🚇 F5 ✉ Pepsi Trocadero, Piccadilly Circus, W1 ☎ 0171 416 6020 🕐 Sun–Thu 10–midnight; Fri–Sat 10AM–1AM) 🍴 Restaurant, cafés 🚇 Piccadilly Circus 💷 Entry free; rides expensive; day-long Adrenalin ticket

POLLOCK TOY MUSEUM

Two houses full of dolls, teddy bears, puppets, and Mr. Pollock's workshop, where he made his toy theaters—still sold at the shop.

🚇 F4 ✉ 1 Scala Street, W1 ☎ 0171 636 3452 🕐 Mon–Sat 10–5. Closed Dec 24–26, Jan 1, public holidays 🚇 Goodge Street 💷 Cheap

ROCK CIRCUS

Rock legends past and present seem to come alive when visitors' headphones pick up infra-red signals and play their songs.

🚇 F5 ✉ London Pavilion, Piccadilly Circus, W1 ☎ 0171 734 7203 🕐 Mon, Wed–Thu, Sun 11–9; Tue 12–9; Fri–Sat 11–10. Closed Dec 25 🚇 Piccadilly Circus 💷 Very expensive; family ticket. Discount tickets for Madame Tussaud's (see opposite) available here

SEGAWORLD

See Pepsi Trocadero, above.

TOWER HILL PAGEANT

A car glides slowly past 26 tableaux of London, giving its sounds, smells and history—an excellent introduction to the City.

🚇 K5 ✉ 1 Tower Hill, Terrace, EC3 ☎ 0171 709 0081 🕐 Apr–Jul, Sep–Oct daily 9:30–5:50. Aug daily 9:30–6. Nov–Mar daily 9:30–4:30. Closed Dec 25 🚇 Tower Hill 🚢 Riverboat to Tower Pier 💷 Expensive; family ticket

TOY WORLD, HARRODS

Up on the fourth floor, this is every child's dream outing. There are plenty of toys that children may play with.

🚇 D7 ✉ Brompton Road, SW1 ☎ 0171 730 1234 🕐 Mon–Sat 10–6; Wed–Fri 10–7. Closed Sun 🍴 Restaurants, cafés 🚇 Knightsbridge 💷 Free

Harrods—an outing in itself

London for free

London has plenty of free activities for all ages. Several public galleries are free (National Gallery ➤ 39, National Portrait Gallery ➤ 38, Tate Gallery, free except for special exhibitions, ➤ 34) plus the commercial ones (➤ 72). Many museums are free (British Museum ➤ 43, Wallace Collection ➤ 51, Bank of England ➤ 50) and music can be enjoyed in church concerts, pubs, and arts complexes. For free theater, try an art auction (➤ 72), a debate in Parliament (➤ 36) or a B.B.C. recording session (☎ 0181 743 8000 and ask for ticket enquiries, specifying radio or TV).

HIDDEN LONDON

Cricket

Anyone who watches or plays cricket should visit the M.C.C. Museum hidden away at Lord's. The story of the game is told in pictures, cartoons, and old battered bats; the Ashes are kept here, too. It is open to ticket-holders on match days, while at other times the guided tour includes the Long Room and the beautiful new stand designed by Michael Hopkins in 1985–87.

➕ D3 ✉ Marylebone Cricket Club, Lord's Ground, NW8 ☎ 0171 289 1611. Tour bookings: 0171 432 1033 🕐 Guided tours: daily 12, 2; match days 10AM, 12, 2; major match days none 🚇 St. John's Wood 🎟 Expensive

See Top 25 Sights for
BANQUETING HOUSE (➤ 37)

CHELSEA PHYSIC GARDEN
Sir Hans Sloane laid out this walled garden for the Society of Apothecaries in 1673.
➕ D8 ✉ Swan Walk, SW3 ☎ 0171 352 5646 🕐 Apr–Oct Wed 2–5; Sun 2–6. 🍴 Tea available 🚇 Sloane Square 🎟 Moderate

DULWICH PICTURE GALLERY ➤ 50

INNER AND MIDDLE TEMPLE
These two Inns of Court are named after the Knights Templar, whose church (➤ 55) is here, too.
➕ H5 ✉ Middle Temple, Middle Temple Lane, EC4 ☎ 0171 427 4800 🕐 Middle Temple Hall: Mon–Fri 10–11:30, 3–4:30 (phone first). Closed Easter, Whitsun, Aug and Christmas 🚇 Temple 🎟 Free

ROYAL HOSPITAL, CHELSEA
Wren's 1682 building, inspired by the Hôtel des Invalides in Paris, is still a home for veteran soldiers.
➕ E8 ✉ Royal Hospital Road, SW3 ☎ 0171 730 0161 🕐 Museum, Great Hall and Chapel: Mon–Fri 10–noon, 2–4; Sat 2–4. Closed public holidays and May 15–end Jun 🚇 Sloane Square 🎟 Free

ST. DUNSTAN IN THE EAST
Wren's 1698 tower soars above a secret garden.
➕ K5 ✉ St. Dunstan's Hill, EC3 🕐 Mon–Fri dawn–dusk 🚇 Monument or Tower Hill 🎟 Free

ST. ETHELDREDA'S ➤ 55

Chelsea Pensioners, residents of the Royal Hospital, Chelsea

ST. GEORGE, HANOVER SQUARE GARDENS
Tree-shaded oasis in Mayfair.
➕ E5 ✉ Enter from South Audley Street and Mount Street, W1 🚇 Bond Street, Green Park 🎟 Free

SUTTON HOUSE
Tudor house (1535) with linen-fold paneling and wall-paintings.
➕ M1 ✉ 2 & 4 Homerton Street, E9 ☎ 0181 986 2264 🕐 Feb–Nov Wed, Sun; public holiday Mon 11:30–5. Mid-Apr–Oct Sat 2–5. Closed Sat Oct 14–Nov 🍴 Café 🚇 Homerton 🎟 Cheap

TEMPLE OF MITHRAS
The ground floor of this Roman temple survives.
➕ J5 ✉ Bucklersbury, EC4 🕐 24 hours 🚇 Bank 🎟 Free

LONDON
where to...

Brasseries & Brunch

The cost of a meal

Eating out in London is generally expensive and prices vary widely. The restaurants on the following pages are in three approximate categories:

£££ from £35 per person, without drinks

££ from £25 per person, without drinks

£ from £12 per person, without drinks.

Service charges (usually 10–12.5 percent) and sometimes cover charges (approximately £1.50 per person) may, or may not, be included.

Museum restaurants

Museum restaurants have improved hugely over recent years. The best are the Tate Restaurant (➤ 34), the Blue Print above the Design Museum (➤ 50) or, simpler, the National Gallery's Brasserie (➤ 39), overlooking Trafalgar Square, and its basement café. The Royal Academy has its restaurant decorated by Academicians (➤ 51). Kensington Palace offers the ultimate tea in its magnificent Orangery (➤ 25); and the Courtauld Institute's tiny café provides delicious soups (➤ 41).

THE BOX (£)
Popular café whose food ranges from *bruschetta pissaladière* to smoked chicken; Sun Box brunch.
🔠 G5 ✉ 32–34 Monmouth Street, WC2 ☎ 0171 240 5828 🕐 Lunch, tea, dinner; Sun brunch 🚇 Covent Garden

BRASSERIE DU MARCHÉ AUX PUCES (££)
At the north end of Portobello Road, ideal after Portobello Market.
🔠 B5 ✉ 349 Portobello Road, W10 ☎ 0181 968 5828 🕐 Breakfast, lunch, dinner 🚇 Ladbroke Grove

LA BRASSERIE ST. QUENTIN (££)
Uncompromisingly French, ideal for an indulgent break from a South Kensington Museums day.
🔠 D7 ✉ 243 Brompton Road, SW3 ☎ 0171 581 5131 🕐 Lunch, dinner 🚇 South Kensington

CAMDEN BRASSERIE (££)
Good for grilled steak, *frites* and a bottle of wine after Camden Lock markets.
🔠 F2 ✉ 214–216 Camden High Street, NW1 ☎ 0171 482 2114 🕐 Lunch, dinner; Sun brunch 🚇 Camden Town

CHRISTOPHER'S (££)
One of the best London haunts for a genuine American brunch, and in one of the capital's most beautiful dining rooms.
🔠 G5 ✉ 18 Wellington Street, WC2 ☎ 0171 240 4222 🕐 Lunch, dinner; Sat, Sun brunch 🚇 Aldwych or Covent Garden

GRILL ST QUENTIN (££)
Good atmosphere in this huge basement where a bowl of *frites* is essential; cheap pre-8PM menu.
🔠 D7 ✉ 2 Yeoman's Row, SW3 ☎ 0171 581 8377 🕐 Lunch, dinner 🚇 South Kensington

JOE ALLEN (££)
A dependably convivial, club-like atmosphere, with healthy American Cal-Ital food served by smiling waiters; reservations essential.
🔠 G5 ✉ 13 Exeter Street, WC2 ☎ 0171 836 0651/497 2148 🕐 Lunch, dinner; Sat, Sun brunch 🚇 Covent Garden

ROYAL GARDEN HOTEL, THE TENTH (£££)
Paul Farr, ex-chef of Claridge's and Mezzo, produces lovely food to match the park views.
🔠 C6 ✉ 2–24 Kensington High Street, W8 ☎ 0171 361 1910 🕐 Lunch, dinner. Closed Sat 🚇 High Street Kensington

SMOLLENSKY'S ON THE STRAND (££)
The large bar is one of London's best; steaks are the thing to eat. Cheap pre-6PM menu.
🔠 G5 ✉ 105 The Strand, WC2 ☎ 0171 497 2101 🕐 Lunch, tea, dinner; Sun brunch 🚇 Charing Cross

WINDOWS ON THE WORLD (£££)
The view is included in the price, as is the skill of chef David Chambers. On a clear day brunch here is memorable.
🔠 E6 ✉ The Hilton Hotel, 22 Park Lane, W1 ☎ 0171 493 8000 🕐 Lunch, dinner; Sun brunch 🚇 Hyde Park Corner

SHOPS & PUBS

CAFÉ AT HEAL'S (££)
Ambrose Heal's store, which promotes vernacular furniture, keeps design as high priority in the café, too; book for lunch.
🔷 F4 ✉ 196 Tottenham Court Road, W1 ☎ 0171 636 1666
🕐 Lunch, tea 🚇 Goodge Street

THE EAGLE (£)
This, the first of London's new-wave pubs (opened 1991), serves robust, Mediterranean food to a noisy full house.
🔷 H4 ✉ 159 Farringdon Road, EC1 ☎ 0171 837 1353
🕐 Lunch, dinner. Closed Sun 🚇 Farringdon

FIFTH FLOOR AT HARVEY NICHOLS (££)
Henry Harris cooks modern British cuisine for a chic clientele in Julian Wickham's designer room. For the less well-heeled, there are two other cafés.
🔷 E6 ✉ Knightsbridge, SW1 ☎ 0171 235 5250 🕐 Lunch, dinner. Closed Sun dinner
🚇 Knightsbridge

HARRODS (£–££)
Each day, 19 eateries swing into action. The best are the Health Juice Bar (basement); the Salt Beef Bar, Champagne and Oyster Bar, Café Espresso and Bar à Fromage (first floor); the Georgian Restaurant and Terrace Bar (good for traditional tea, 5th floor); and the Ice-cream Parlour and Upper Circle Self-Service.
🔷 D7 ✉ Knightsbridge, SW1 ☎ 0171 730 1234
🕐 Breakfast, lunch, tea 🚇 Knightsbridge

LAMB TAVERN (£)
Regulars claim this restored Victorian pub in the Leadenhall Market serves the best hot roast beef sandwiches in the City.
🔷 K5 ✉ 10–12 Leadenhall Market, EC3 ☎ 0171 626 2454
🕐 Lunch. Closed Sat, Sun 🚇 Bank or Monument

LIBERTY'S (£–££)
It is almost a meal just feasting on the goods in this exotic store; in case not, the stylish ABC Café is the best of three options.
🔷 F5 ✉ 214–22 Regent Street, W1 ☎ 0171 734 1234
🕐 Breakfast, lunch, tea 🚇 Oxford Circus

NEWMAN ARMS (£)
The pie room upstairs is what this pub is all about, with fillings ranging from steak and kidney or fish to lamb and rosemary; the salads are equally delicious.
🔷 F4 ✉ 23 Rathbone Street, W1 ☎ 0171 336 1127
🕐 Mon–Fri lunch 🚇 Goodge Street

PEASANT (£)
A pub touched with the wand of a design-conscious foodie. Its modern Italian food is excellent. Well located for the City and Barbican.
🔷 H4 ✉ 240 St. John Street, EC1 ☎ 0171 336 7726
🕐 Lunch, dinner. Closed Sat lunch, Sun 🚇 Farringdon

SCARSDALE (£)
Pretty Kensington pub with a garden overlooking Edwardes Square, serving traditional pub food.
🔷 B7 ✉ 23a Edwardes Square, W8 ☎ 0171 937 1811
🕐 Lunch, dinner 🚇 High Street Kensington

Fish restaurants
With the increased popularity of fish, most London restaurants are cooking it better and some—often devoted to fish—very well. For traditional recipes try Sweetings in the City (✉ 39 Queen Victoria Street) or Green's Restaurant and Oyster Bar (✉ 36 Duke Street, St. James's). (The English oyster season covers all the months with an 'r' in them.) Less formal are the very jolly Manzi's (➤ 86), L'Altro (➤ 68), Livebait (✉ 43 The Cut, SE1), and Sheekey's Brasserie (✉ 28 St. Martin's Court). For good fish and chips, try Wilton Road, behind Victoria Station.

BREAKFAST & TEA

Set-price menus

Most of London's pricier restaurants offer two set-price menus, the cheaper at lunchtime. Stick to them and you can savor sublime dishes. Consider dressing up to try classic Anglo-French cuisine at the exquisite Connaught Grill (➤ 69), or spend an afternoon lunching at Pierre Koffman's La Tante Claire (➤ 65). All the star chefs offer these menus, from Alastair Little (➤ 69) and Gordon Ramsay (➤ 65) to Bruno Loubet and even Marco Pierrre White and Michel Roux (all ➤ 65).

The check

A good-value menu can be transformed into an outrageous check if you do not look sharp. Check beforehand whether or not service, VAT and coffee are included, and order tap water if you do not want to pay for bottled. When the check arrives, look it over carefully. If service is already added, you are not obliged to leave a tip, even if the waiter looks hopeful.

CAFÉ DE PARIS (£)
The Pyramid Tea Dance is the real thing: ballroom and Latin dancing classics plus full afternoon tea.
✚ G5 ✉ 3 Coventry Street, W1 ☎ 0171 734 7700
🕐 Sun tea 🚇 Piccadilly Circus
❓ Dress code: dancing

CLARIDGE'S (££)
Breakfast is in the immaculate art deco restaurant; tea, the best in London, is taken on sofas in the foyer alcove—reservations essential.
✚ E5 ✉ Brook Street, W1 ☎ 0171 629 8860
🕐 Breakfast, tea 🚇 Bond Street ❓ Dress code: jacket and tie

COFFEE GALLERY (£)
Italian-run café, ideal for pre-British Museum coffee and croissants, and post-museum pasta and wicked cakes.
✚ G5 ✉ 23 Museum Street, WC1 ☎ 0171 436 0455
🕐 Breakfast, tea. Closed Sun
🚇 Leicester Square

FOUNDATION AT HARVEY NICHOLS (££)
Chic, cool basement, as design-aware as the five floors of fashion above it.
✚ E6 ✉ Knightsbridge (Saville Street entrance), SW1 ☎ 0171 201 8000
🕐 Breakfast, lunch, tea
🚇 Knightsbridge

FOX AND ANCHOR (£)
Join the Smithfield meat-market workers for a full English breakfast washed down with coffee (or a pint). Best value in town.
✚ J4 ✉ 115 Charterhouse Street, EC1 ☎ 0171 253 4838
🕐 Breakfast. Closed Sun
🚇 Barbican or Farringdon

HYDE PARK HOTEL (££)
Reserve a window table in the Park Room for a stylish breakfast or tea overlooking Hyde Park.
✚ E6 ✉ Knightsbridge, SW1 ☎ 0171 235 2000
🕐 Breakfast, tea 🚇 Hyde Park Corner

PÂTISSERIE VALERIE (£)
Coffee, croissants and cakes at tiny tables in the original café-shop. Six branches.
✚ F5 ✉ 44 Old Compton Street, W1 ☎ 0171 437 3466
🕐 Breakfast, tea 🚇 Leicester Square or Tottenham Court Road

SAVOY HOTEL (££)
Book a window table for breakfast in the River Room; tea is on sofas in the pretty Thames Foyer.
✚ G5 ✉ Strand, WC2 ☎ 0171 836 4343
🕐 Breakfast, tea 🚇 Aldwych
❓ Dress code: jacket and tie

SIMPSON'S-IN-THE-STRAND (££)
Glorious setting for a traditional breakfast—such as porridge followed by kippers or kidneys.
✚ G5 ✉ 100 Strand, WC2 ☎ 0171 836 9112
🕐 Breakfast, tea 🚇 Aldwych
❓ Dress code: jacket and tie

WALDORF HOTEL (££)
Breakfast in the lofty Palm Court is buffet-style; tea is traditional, with weekend tea-dances.
✚ G5 ✉ Aldwych, WC2 ☎ 0171 836 2400
🕐 Breakfast, tea 🚇 Aldwych
❓ Dress code: jacket and tie for tea-dance

FAMOUS CHEFS

**RICHARD CORRIGAN:
SEARCY'S BRASSERIE
(££)**

Masterly modern British
dishes—before and after
the Barbican shows.

J4 ✉ Barbican Centre, Silk
Street, EC2 ☎ 0171 588 3008
🕐 Lunch, dinner. Closed Sat
lunch, Sun dinner 🚇 Barbican

**PIERRE KOFFMANN: LA
TANTE CLAIRE (£££)**

Enter culinary heaven for
a meal created by this
three-star Michelin chef.

E8 ✉ 68 Royal Hospital
Road, SW3 ☎ 0171 352 6045
🕐 Lunch, dinner. Closed Sat, Sun
🚇 Sloane Square

**ROWLEY LEIGH:
KENSINGTON PLACE
(££)**

Top-notch food at
reasonable prices in west
London's noisiest, jolliest
upscale social restaurant.

B6 ✉ 201–205 Kensington
Church Street, W8 ☎ 0171
727 3184 🕐 Lunch, dinner
🚇 Notting Hill Gate

**BRUNO LOUBET:
L'ODÉON (£££)**

Robust perfection in a
large yet intimate setting.

F5 ✉ 65 Regent Street, W1
☎ 0171 287 1400 🕐 Lunch,
dinner 🚇 Picadilly Circus

**JEAN-CHRISTOPHE
NOVELLI: MAISON
NOVELLI (£££)**

Well worth bypassing the
brasserie for the pricier
upstairs restaurant.

H4 ✉ 29 Clerkenwell Green,
EC1 ☎ 0171 251 6606
🕐 Lunch, dinner. Closed Sat, Sun
🚇 Farringdon

**GORDON RAMSAY:
AUBERGINE (£££)**

French food that uses
ingredients such as truffle
oil over the haricots blancs.

C8 ✉ 11 Park Walk, SW10
☎ 0171 352 3449 🕐 Lunch,
dinner. Closed Sat lunch, Sun
🚇 South Kensington or
Gloucester Road

**RUTH ROGERS AND
ROSE GRAY: RIVER
CAFÉ (£££)**

Outstanding modern
Italian food in Richard
Rogers's refurbished room.

Off map at A8 ✉ Thames
Wharf, Rainville Road, W6
☎ 0171 381 8824 🕐 Lunch,
dinner. Closed Sun dinner
🚇 Hammersmith

**MICHEL ROUX: LA
GAVROCHE (£££)**

Albert's son sticks to
classic French, but lighter.

E5 ✉ 43 Upper Brook
Street, W1 ☎ 0171 408 0881
🕐 Lunch, dinner. Closed Sat, Sun
🚇 Oxford Circus

**JOHN TORODE: MEZZO
(£££)**

Impressive food and
service in a vast, noisy,
trendy ex-nightclub.

F5 ✉ 100 Wardour Street,
W1 ☎ 0171 314 4000
🕐 Lunch, dinner. Closed Sat lunch
🚇 Leicester Square

**MARCO PIERRE
WHITE: THE
RESTAURANT, HYDE
PARK HOTEL (£££)**

In posh Knightsbridge,
the *enfant terrible* harasses
his clients less—but still
cooks wonderfully. You
can also taste his food, at
arm's length, at the
Criterion, Piccadilly.

E6 ✉ 66 Knightsbridge,
SW1 ☎ 0171 235 2000/
259 5380 🕐 Lunch, dinner.
Closed Sat lunch, Sun 🚇 Hyde
Park Corner

Riverside eating

London has only recently
cottoned on to the potential of its
riverside views. Today there is
more than just the grand Savoy
River Room (➤ 64) and the
East End smugglers' pubs
(➤ 57). The most spectacular
views are from the Oxo Tower
Restaurant (✉ Barge House
Street, SE1 ☎ 0171 803
3888)—serious food, views,
and prices. Next best are the
views from the first-floor Blue
Print Café, beside the Design
Museum, Butler's Wharf,
overlooking Tower Bridge and
the City (➤ 50). For more
modest river-view eating, try
Embankment Tea House, on a
mound in Victoria Embankment
Gardens, and Barley Mow pub
(✉ 44 Narrow Street, E14),
whose outdoor tables overlook
the wider, curving Thames of
the East End.

CHINESE & FAR EASTERN RESTAURANTS

Best settings

If part of the pleasure of dining out is the setting, London has much to offer. For grandeur, there's the Ritz (➤ 84) at lunchtime; for sparkle, the mosaic-clad Criterion (Piccadilly); for art deco, Claridge's (➤ 84); for *fin de siècle*, the Café Royal (✉ Regent Street, W1). There are wacky settings, such as Balti's (➤ 67), the Dorchester's pricey Oriental (✉ Park Lane, W1) and the Star of India (➤ 67). And there are atmospheric pubs such as the George Inn (✉ 77 Borough High Street, SE1), architects' dreams such as the River Café and Oxo Tower Restaurant (both ➤ 65) and the most beautiful walls at Christopher's (➤ 62).

ABENO (££)
A ten-minute walk from Colindale Underground station, this *okonomi-yaki* (mini-pizzas cooked on a griddle) restaurant is in Europe's only Japanese shopping plaza.
➕ Off map at A1 ✉ Yaohan Plaza, 339 Edgware Road, NW9 ☎ 0181 205 1131 🕐 Lunch, dinner 🚇 Colindale

BAHN THAI (££)
The finest Thai cooking in London, for price and authenticity; reserve a table on the first floor.
➕ F5 ✉ 21a Frith Street, W1 ☎ 0171 437 8504 🕐 Lunch, dinner 🚇 Tottenham Court Road

CHURCHILL ARMS (£)
London's first pub to serve good, inexpensive Thai food. Best to book.
➕ B6 ✉ 119 Kensington Church Street, W8 ☎ 0171 792 1246 🕐 Lunch, dinner. Closed Sun dinner 🚇 Notting Hill Gate

FUNG SHING (££)
Consistently good Cantonese dishes; follow the manager's advice.
➕ G5 ✉ 15 Lisle Street, WC2 ☎ 0171 437 1539 🕐 Lunch, dinner 🚇 Leicester Square

HARBOUR CITY (£)
Great *dim sum* in a highly reputed Soho Chinese restaurant.
➕ G5 ✉ 46 Gerrard Street, W1 ☎ 0171 439 7859 🕐 Lunch, dinner 🚇 Leicester Square

IMPERIAL CITY (££)
Good Chinese food in the Royal Exchange vaults.
➕ K5 ✉ Royal Exchange, Cornhill, EC3 ☎ 0171 626 3437 🕐 Lunch, dinner. Closed Sat, Sun 🚇 Bank

MANOROM (£)
Unusually for Covent Garden, this small, efficient restaurant serves good food at low prices; keep off the set-price menu.
➕ G5 ✉ 16 Maiden Lane, WC2 ☎ 0171 240 4139 🕐 Lunch, dinner. Closed Sat lunch, Sun 🚇 Leicester Square

ROYAL CHINA (££)
Book a table or join the justifiably long lines for the best *dim sum* in town.
➕ C5 ✉ 13 Queensway, W2 ☎ 0171 221 2535 🕐 Lunch, dinner. No booking Sat, Sun 🚇 Queensway

SINGAPORE GARDEN (££)
A favorite with north Londoners, and always packed, for its Malaysian and Indonesian seasonal specialties. Branch in Gloucester Place.
➕ C2 ✉ 83—83a Fairfax Road, NW6 ☎ 0171 328 5314 🕐 Lunch, dinner 🚇 Swiss Cottage

VONG (£££)
Jean-Georges Vongerichten, from Alsace via New York, fuses French and Thai cuisines.
➕ E6 ✉ The Berkeley Hotel, Wilton Place, SW1 ☎ 0171 235 1010 🕐 Lunch, dinner. Closed Sun 🚇 Hyde Park Corner

WAGAMAMA (£)
London's trendiest Japanese *ramen* bar, convenient for the British Museum. Branch in Lexington Street, W1.
➕ G5 ✉ 4 Streatham Street, WC1 ☎ 0171 323 9223 🕐 Lunch, dinner. No booking 🚇 Tottenham Court Road

INDIAN & VEGETARIAN RESTAURANTS

CAFÉ SPICE NAMASTE (£)

Cyrus Todiwala's food is good and his setting very jolly; good for after a visit to the Tower of London.

L5 ☒ 16 Prescot Street, E1 ☎ 0171 488 9242 ⏰ Lunch, dinner. Closed Sat lunch, Sun Ⓜ Aldgate

CHUTNEY MARY (££)

Try unusual Indian recipes from Goa, Kerala, and other little-known regional cuisines.

C9 ☒ 535 King's Road, SW10 ☎ 0171 351 3113 ⏰ Lunch, dinner. Sun buffet lunch Ⓜ Fulham Broadway

CRANKS (£)

The mother of London veggie restaurants and one of a chain serving good-value, good-quality food. Covent Garden and Great Newport Street branches are open Sun.

F5 ☒ 8 Marshall Street, W1 ☎ 0171 437 9431 ⏰ Breakfast, lunch, dinner (8–8). Closed Sun Ⓜ Oxford Circus

DIWANA BHEL POORI HOUSE (£)

Bhel poori are fried snacks sold on the Bombay streets and beaches; in this vegetarian restaurant they are served as first courses.

F4 ☒ 121 Drummond Street, NW1 ☎ 0171 387 5556 ⏰ Lunch, dinner. Lunch buffet. No booking; for dinner bring your own alcohol Ⓜ Euston

MANDEER (£)

Gentle Gujarati and richer Punjabi dishes, all vegetarian. Order a *thali*, or complete meal.

F5 ☒ 21 Hannay Place, W1 ☎ 0171 323 0660 ⏰ Lunch, dinner. Closed Sun Ⓜ Tottenham Court Road

SALLOOS (££)

Upscale, good North-West Frontier food for meat-eaters, cooked by Mr Salahuddin of Lahore.

E6 ☒ 62–4 Kinnerton Street, SW1 ☎ 0171 235 4444 ⏰ Lunch, dinner. Closed Sun Ⓜ Hyde Park Corner

STAR OF INDIA (££)

Reza's panache and Vineet's cooking create a total experience like no other in London—or India.

C8 ☒ 154 Old Brompton Road, SW5 ☎ 0171 373 2901 ⏰ Lunch, dinner Ⓜ Gloucester Road

SWEET AND SPICY (£)

Basic cafeteria-style eatery serving Pakistani food, mostly to local Bangladeshis.

L4 ☒ 40 Brick Lane, E1 ☎ 0171 247 1081 ⏰ Breakfast, lunch, tea, dinner Ⓜ Shoreditch

TAMARIND (££)

Atul Kochhar combs Indian villages from Uttar Pradesh to Kerala to find traditional local recipes.

E6 ☒ 20 Queen Street, W1 ☎ 0171 629 3561 ⏰ Lunch, dinner. Closed Sat lunch Ⓜ Green Park

WORLD FOOD CAFÉ (£)

A fresh, modern approach to vegetarian food, with Indian, Mexican, Greek, and Turkish influences.

G5 ☒ First floor, 14 Neal's Yard, WC2 ☎ 0171 379 0298 ⏰ Mon–Sat lunch; Wed–Fri dinner until 8PM (May–Sep only). No booking; bring your own alcohol Ⓜ Covent Garden

Indian food

An Indian meal should have many dishes, so if there is a group of you it is best to make a collective order and share. Tandoori dishes (cooked in a clay oven) make a good start. The main course dishes should arrive together: one or two meat, two or three vegetable, a lentil or pulse dish (such as chickpeas), rice and a variety of breads such as *chapati* or *nan*—which are eaten hot, so order more as you go along. Remember the yogurt and pickles, and drink *lassi* (a buttermilk or yogurt drink that comes in sweet or salty versions) or beer. Vegetarians will find a good range of food, mild and spicy, in London's 2,000 Indian restaurants.

ITALIAN & FRENCH RESTAURANTS

American food

America's fast food arrived long before its quality cuisine and restaurant style. However, the newer arrivals have made up for lost time and there are now plenty of places to hang out: The Hard Rock Café (✉ 150 Old Park Lane, W1), Kenny's (✉ 2a Pond Place, SW3), Rock Island Diner (✉ Plaza Centre, London Pavilion, Piccadilly), Planet Hollywood (✉ Trocadero Centre, Coventry Street, W1), Fatboy's Diner (✉ 21 Maiden Lane, WC2), Chicago Pizza Pie Factory (✉ 17 Hanover Square, W1), TGIF (✉ 6 Bedford Street and branches), and more. PJ's Grill (✉ 52 Fulham Road, SW3) and Smollensky's (▶ 62) are slightly upscale; Joe Allen (▶ 62) and Christopher's (▶ 62) are a lot more so, while Clarke's (✉ 124 Kensington Church Street, W8) sits at the top.

AL SAN VINCENZO (££)
Essential to book one of the few tables to enjoy Neapolitan Signore Borgonzolo's cooking.
➕ D5 ✉ 30 Connaught Street, W2 ☎ 0171 262 9623 🕐 Lunch, dinner. Closed Sat lunch, Sun 🚇 Marble Arch

BERTORELLI'S (££)
A Covent Garden favorite; good buzz and food, and efficient enough to cope with the pre- or post-opera rush from across the way.
➕ G5 ✉ 44a Floral Street, WC2 ☎ 0171 836 3969 🕐 Lunch, dinner 🚇 Covent Garden

BOUDIN BLANC (££)
Extremely good-value French food, especially considering its Mayfair setting in Shepherd Market. There's also a cheap pre-8PM menu.
➕ E6 ✉ 5 Trebeck Street, W1 ☎ 0171 499 3292 🕐 Lunch, dinner 🚇 Green Park

CAFÉ DU MARCHÉ (££)
In the cobblestone mews in the square's west corner, this rustic French restaurant has a laid-back pianist each evening.
➕ J4 ✉ 22 Charterhouse Square, EC1 ☎ 0171 608 1609 🕐 Lunch, dinner. Closed Sat lunch, Sun 🚇 Barbican

CHEZ MAX (££)
At the West Brompton end of Fulham Road, classic French food from the Renzland brothers—at West End prices.
➕ C8 ✉ 168 Ifield Road, SW10 ☎ 0171 835 0874 🕐 Lunch, dinner. Closed Mon lunch, Sun 🚇 West Brompton

L'ALTRO (££)
Fashionable Kensington restaurant serving Italian seafood on earthenware platters; much patronized by locals.
➕ A5 ✉ 210 Kensington Park Road, W11 ☎ 0171 792 1066/1077 🕐 Lunch, dinner 🚇 Ladbroke Grove

L'ARTÉ (£)
Modern Italian cooking at low prices, with an all-Italian wine list.
➕ F4 ✉ 126 Cleveland Street, W1 ☎ 0171 813 1011 🕐 Lunch, dinner. Closed Sat lunch, Sun 🚇 Great Portland Street

PALAIS DU JARDIN (££)
Good atmosphere and food in a huge stylish brasserie, with tables outside in summer.
➕ G5 ✉ 136 Long Acre, WC2 ☎ 0171 379 5353 🕐 Lunch, dinner 🚇 Leicester Square or Covent Garden

PIZZA EXPRESS (£)
Located in a tiled Victorian dairy. A branch of the reliable Pizza Express chain, whose pizzas have thin crispy crusts and good toppings.
➕ G5 ✉ 30 Coptic Street, WC1 ☎ 0171 636 3232 🕐 Lunch, dinner 🚇 Tottenham Court Road or Holborn

SPAGHETTI HOUSE (£)
Still Italian-run, this is one of 20 branches in London serving good pasta, meat and fish at low prices in pleasant surroundings.
➕ F4 ✉ 15–17 Goodge Street, W1 ☎ 0171 636 6582 🕐 Lunch, dinner. Closed Sun lunch 🚇 Goodge Street

ENGLISH RESTAURANTS

ALASTAIR LITTLE: LANCASTER ROAD (££)

If Alastair Little's plate-glassed Soho showpiece is beyond the purse, come to this less formal but highly fashionable outpost.

➕ A5 ✉ 136a Lancaster Road, W11 ☎ 0171 243 2000 🕐 Lunch, dinner. Closed Sun 🚇 Ladbroke Grove

ATLANTIC BAR AND GRILL (££)

A big, lofty basement in the Regent Palace Hotel off Piccadilly Circus; good bar, which attracts a trendy clientele.

➕ F5 ✉ 20 Glasshouse Street, W1 ☎ 0171 734 4888 🕐 Lunch, dinner. Closed lunch Sat and Sun 🚇 Piccadilly Circus ❓ Dress code: trendy

THE CONNAUGHT (£££)

Whether you choose the more public restaurant or the pale green Grill Room at the back, all is quintessentially English.

➕ E5 ✉ Carlos Place, W1 ☎ 0171 499 7070 🕐 Lunch, dinner 🚇 Bond Street ❓ Dress code: jacket and tie

FRENCH HOUSE DINING ROOM (££)

Cozy dining-room over a Soho pub serving modern dishes. Its Clerkenwell outpost is the St. John.

➕ F5 ✉ 45 Dean Street, W1 ☎ 0171 437 2477 🕐 Lunch, dinner. Closed Sun 🚇 Tottenham Court Road

THE IVY (££)

A revived theaterland classic with artworks by Peter Blake and Howard Hodgkin on the walls, celebrities galore and modern British food.

➕ G5 ✉ 1 West Street, WC2 ☎ 0171 836 4751 🕐 Lunch, dinner 🚇 Leicester Square

LEITH'S (£££)

Go for the imaginative modern British food, with plenty of vegetarian dishes, not for the new, sterile décor.

➕ A5 ✉ 92 Kensington Park Road, W11 ☎ 0171 229 4481 🕐 Lunch, dinner. Closed Sat–Mon lunch, Sun dinner 🚇 Notting Hill Gate

RULES (££)

Founded in 1798, one of London's oldest restaurants; reliable traditional food in its plush Edwardian rooms.

➕ G5 ✉ 35 Maiden Lane, WC2 ☎ 0171 836 5314 🕐 Lunch, dinner 🚇 Covent Garden

SIMPSON'S (££)

Opened in 1848 as Simpson's Divan and Tavern, where chess players lolled on divans to feast on roast beef. Today, there's just the roast beef and other traditional dishes.

➕ G5 ✉ 110 Strand, WC2 ☎ 0171 836 9112 🕐 Breakfast, lunch, dinner 🚇 Aldwych ❓ Dress code: jacket and tie

STEPHEN BULL (££)

Stephen Bull's original, rather spartan restaurant delivers robust, modern British food. There's a Bistro branch in Clerkenwell, with a seafood bar.

➕ E5 ✉ 7 Blandford Street, W1 ☎ 0171 486 9696 🕐 Lunch, dinner. Closed Sat lunch, Sun 🚇 Baker Street

English cuisine

English cuisine may be derided, but there is in fact both fine traditional and impressive new wave cooking to be enjoyed, though it is not cheap.

Eat as much as you can buffet deals

Unlimited food at a fixed price may be essential for families with growing children—or simply for hungry adults. The Waldorf Hotel's buffet breakfast makes a good start to the day (➤ 64). Many larger hotels, such as the Basil Street (➤ 85), do the equivalent but at lunchtime. Sunday lunch buffets in Indian restaurants are fun.

Shopping Areas

Regular store hours are 9:30 or 10AM until between 5:30 and 7PM, with late-night shopping in Knightsbridge on Wednesdays and Oxford Street, Regent Street and Covent Garden on Thursdays.

Tax-free goods

If you are a non-U.K. passport holder, consider the VAT Retails Export Scheme. VAT (Value Added Tax) is rated at 17½ percent in Britain and payable on almost everything except books, food and children's clothes. All non-U.K. passport holders are exempt from VAT if they are taking the goods out of the country within three months. The tax must be paid first, then claimed back. You must have your passport and return ticket with you; the shop assistant will help you complete the form VAT407—make sure you keep your part of it along with the export sales bill. Show Customs this form and have your goods ready to show.

London's stores tend to be found in clusters; conserve your energy and shop in one area.

BOND STREET
Bond Street mixes haute-couture outlets with art galleries. Asprey's, one of the world's great luxury stores, is here, as are the Fine Art Society and Sotheby's.
F5 ⊠ Mayfair, W1
ⓔ Bond Street or Green Park

BROMPTON CROSS
Sophisticated fashion and design stores. The Conran store, selling quality design, is the longest-established store.
D7 ⊠ Knightsbridge/Chelsea, SW3 ⓔ Knightsbridge or South Kensington

JERMYN STREET
Once the local street for aristocrats swarming round St. James's Palace; the atmosphere of Jermyn Street remains select: Floris the perfumier (est. 1730); Paxton & Whitfield for cheeses; and Harvie and Hudson or Turnbull & Asser for shirts.
F6 ⊠ St. James's, SW1
ⓔ Piccadilly Circus or Green Park

KENSINGTON CHURCH STREET
This once-quiet lane now has more than 50 antiques stores, Clarke's restaurant bakery, Boyd's and Kensington Place.
B6 ⊠ Kensington, W8
ⓔ Notting Hill Gate or High Steet Kensington

NEAL STREET
The epitome of Covent Garden's successful rebirth, this pedestrian street is packed with exotic little stores: Smith's Gallery, Neal Street East, the Kite Store and, in Neal's Yard, a feast of wholefoods.
G5 ⊠ Covent Garden, WC2
ⓔ Covent Garden

OLD COMPTON STREET
In the 18th century, this was the social center for French exiles. Pâtisserie Valerie at no. 44 keeps the mood alive; Italians run the tiny Pollo and Presto bars, Vinorio, Camisa and the newsstand Moroni's.
F5 ⊠ Soho, W1
ⓔ Tottenham Court Road

OXFORD STREET
The capital's main shopping artery. At the west end, Marks & Spencer stocks the chain's greatest variety of clothing; in the middle are Selfridges and branches of all significant chains from Body Shop to Gap, and John Lewis.
E–G5 ⊠ Mayfair/Marylebone, W1 ⓔ Oxford Circus, Bond Street, Marble Arch, Tottenham Court Road

REGENT STREET
With its dramatic curve north from Piccadilly, Nash's street is as smart as intended: Tower Records, Austin Reed, the sumptuous Café Royal, Mappin and Webb (silver), Garrard (jewels), Hamleys (toys), Liberty (► 71) and the Warner Bros and Disney stores. North of Oxford Street lies the excellent B.B.C. store.
F5 ⊠ Mayfair/Soho, W1
ⓔ Piccadilly Circus or Oxford Street

DEPARTMENT STORES

FORTNUM & MASON
Before going in, do not miss the clock, which has Messrs. Fortnum and Mason mincing forward each hour. Prices are high, but the store-brand goods make perfect presents.
🚉 F6 ✉ 181 Piccadilly, W1 ☎ 0171 734 8040 🚇 Piccadilly Circus or Green Park

GENERAL TRADING COMPANY
Quality buys in all departments from china to gardening; excellent mail-order catalogue.
🚉 E7 ✉ 144 Sloane Street, SW1 ☎ 0171 730 0411 🚇 Sloane Square

HARRODS
This vast emporium contains just about everything anyone could want, and 19 places to eat. Apart from the revamaped fashion departments, do not miss the spectacular food halls.
🚉 D6 ✉ Knightsbridge, SW1 ☎ 0171 730 1234 🚇 Knightsbridge

HARVEY NICHOLS
London's classiest clothes store, from its original store-windows to the well-stocked fashion floors.
🚉 E6 ✉ 109–125 Knightsbridge, SW1 ☎ 0171 235 5000 🚇 Knightsbridge

JOHN LEWIS
Its slogan, "never knowingly undersold," inspires a confidence that prices are solidly fair.
🚉 F5 ✉ Oxford Street, W1 ☎ 0171 629 7711 🚇 Oxford Circus

LIBERTY
This store's quality stock is characterized by exoticism mixed with an Arts and Crafts heritage. Goods on offer range from sumptuous fabrics to the best china and glass.
🚉 F5 ✉ Regent Street, W1 ☎ 0171 734 1234 🚇 Oxford Circus

LILLYWHITES
When the rain comes, this is the place to go and get what you need, either by Aquascutum, or perhaps Barbour, Partridge or Husky; and whatever the sport, this store has the outfit and equipment.
🚉 F5 ✉ Piccadilly Circus, W1 ☎ 0171 930 3181 🚇 Piccadilly Circus

MARKS & SPENCER
Most people buy some thing at M&S. Clothes now have sharper styles, and the food departments are exceptional.
🚉 E5 ✉ 458 Oxford Street, W1 ☎ 0171 935 7954 🚇 Marble Arch

SCOTCH HOUSE
Plaid and more plaid on three floors. Especially good for soft lambswool and cashmere woolens, as well as traditional, quality Scottish clothing.
🚉 D6 ✉ 2 Brompton Road, SW1 ☎ 0171 581 2151 🚇 South Kensington

SELFRIDGES
This vast, bedazzling store stocks beauty goods available nowhere else, prepares food, and creates Christmas window displays that deserve a special night outing.
🚉 E5 ✉ 400 Oxford Street, W1 ☎ 0171 629 1234 🚇 Marble Arch or Bond Street

One-stop shopping
The one-stop shopping that department stores offer has several advantages over schlepping around the streets. If it rains, you stay dry. If you are hungry, there are cafés. There are also the services to be considered. Your purchases from various departments can be held for you while you shop, to be collected together at the end. Garments can be altered, presents wrapped and writing paper printed. And most stores have dependable after-sales service if something is not right.

ART & ANTIQUES

Buying at auction

Watching an auction is one thing; buying is quite another. At the pre-sale viewing, inspect any lot you may bid for and check its description and estimated sale price in the catalogue. If you cannot attend the sale, leave a bid; if you can, decide on your maximum bid and do not go above it! Bid by lifting your hand up high. If successful, pay and collect after the sale, or arrange for delivery.

ANTIQUARIUS
London's oldest antiques center houses 120 dealers whose goods include lace, old clothes and jewelry; there are plenty of quirky, affordable items here.
🚇 D8 ✉ 131–141 King's Road, SW3 ☎ 0171 351 5353 Ⓢ Sloane Square

BONHAM'S
The strength of this auction house (still a family firm) lies in its 20th-century and specialist sales. Cheaper goods are sold in its Chelsea Galleries.
🚇 D7 ✉ Montpelier Galleries, Montpelier Street, SW7 ☎ 0171 584 9161 Ⓢ Knightsbridge

CHRISTIE'S
The auction house has departments ranging from grand Old Masters to coins and tribal art. A second, cheaper sale room is in South Kensington.
🚇 F6 ✉ Christie, Manson & Wood, 8 King Street, SW1 ☎ 0171 839 9060 Ⓢ Green Park

GRAY'S ANTIQUE MARKET
High-quality goods ranging from pictures to silver are sold at 170 stalls.
🚇 E5 ✉ 1–7 Davies Mews and 58 Davies Street, W1 ☎ 0171 629 7034 Ⓢ Bond Street

LEGER GALLERIES
Top English paintings by artists such as Turner and Gainsborough; Agnew's, Colnaghi, Frost & Reed and Philip Mould near by are also worth visiting.
🚇 F6 ✉ 13 Old Bond Street, W1 ☎ 0171 629 3538 Ⓢ Green Park

MALLETT AT BOURDON HOUSE
Highly polished tables, chairs and other furniture exhibited in the rarefied atmosphere of a 1720s house; well worth visiting.
🚇 E5 ✉ 2 Davies Street, W1 ☎ 0171 629 2444 Ⓢ Bond Street

SOTHEBY'S
The world's largest auction house. This is a rabbit-warren of sale rooms with objects of all kinds on view. The "Colonnade" sales are cheaper.
🚇 F5 ✉ 34 New Bond Street, W1 ☎ 0171 493 8080 Ⓢ Bond Street

SPINK & SON
best known for their coins, medals and ravishing silver and watercolors; see also their Indian and Far Eastern department.
🚇 F6 ✉ 5 King Street, SW1 ☎ 0171 930 7888 Ⓢ Green Park

VIGO CARPET GALLERY
A huge stock from all periods, with helpful staff.
🚇 F5 ✉ 6a Vigo Street, W1 ☎ 0171 439 6971 Ⓢ Piccadilly

WADDINGTON GALLERIES
In a small street lined with about 20 galleries selling modern art, Waddington is just one worth seeing; try also Theo Waddington, Redfern, The Gallery and Browse & Darby, and explore nearby Clifford and Derring Streets.
🚇 F5 ✉ 12 and 34 Cork Street, W1 ☎ 0171-437 8611/439 6262 Ⓢ Green Park

CHINA & GLASS

ARAM DESIGNS LTD
Aram's international contemporary design includes works by Depadova.

✚ G5 ✉ 3 Kean Street, WC2 ☎ 0171 240 3933 🚇 Aldwych or Covent Garden

ARIA TABLE ART
Located in trendy Islington, Aria stocks modern international state-of-the-art design, with plenty of Italian pieces on display. There is a second shop across the road devoted to bathroom accessories.

✚ H2 ✉ 133 Upper Street, N1 ☎ 0171 226 1021 🚇 Angel

DESIGNER'S GUILD
Tricia Guild's store is a wonderland of exquisite design. As well as the pieces of contemporary china and glass, you may find her fabrics irresistible.

✚ D8 ✉ 277 King's Road, SW3 ☎ 0171 351 5775 🚇 Sloane Square then 15 minutes' walk or bus 19 or 22

HABITAT
Founded by Sir Terence Conran, this contemporary furniture store stocks a variety of glass, china and household goods.

✚ F4 ✉ 196 Tottenham Court Road, W1 ☎ 0171 631 3880 🚇 Goodge Street

HEAL'S
A frontrunner of the Arts and Crafts movement in the 1920s, Heal's specializes in timeless modern furniture.

✚ F4 ✉ 196 Tottenham Court Road, W1 ☎ 0171 636 1666 🚇 Goodge Street

JEANETTE HAYHURST
This is one of the few places to find old glass, especially British pieces; it also stocks interesting studio glass.

✚ B6 ✉ 32a Kensington Church Street, W8 ☎ 0171 938 1539 🚇 High Street Kensington

REJECT CHINA SHOP
This, the largest branch of the chain, stocks Spode and Denby and plenty of pottery and earthenware, as well as crystal and cutlery.

✚ D7 ✉ 183 Brompton Road, SW3 ☎ 0171 581 0739 🚇 Knightsbridge

RJ HOME SHOP
This cut-price store always has bargains, especially in glass, but inspect the goods carefully.

✚ F4 ✉ 209 Tottenham Court Road, W1 ☎ 0171 580 2895 🚇 Goodge Street

RON ARAD ASSOCIATES
Ron Arad's designs are limited-edition pieces of furniture for the collector.

✚ E2 ✉ 62 Chalk Farm Road, NW1 ☎ 0171 284 4963 🚇 Chalk Farm

WATERFORD WEDGWOOD
The largest selection of hand-made, full lead crystal Waterford glass, all made in Ireland, and Wedgwood china. Will phone the factory for special orders, help customers search for designs no longer made and ship goods worldwide.

✚ F5 ✉ 173–4 Piccadilly, W1 ☎ 0171 629 2614 🚇 Piccadilly Circus

Do not worry about breaking your valuable purchases on the way home; they can be packed and sent there for you, fully insured.

Silver
English silver is one of the best antiques buys because it has been hallmarked since the mid-17th century, so you know precisely what you are buying. To get a good look, wander the London Silver Vaults in Chancery Lane, Antiquarius (➤ 72), Gray's Antique Market (➤ 72), Garrard (➤ 70), and Mappin & Webb (➤ 70). Buy at these locations or visit Christine Schell (✉ 15 Cale Street, SW3) for silver and tortoiseshell, or John Jesse (✉ 160 Kensington Church Street, W8) for art deco.

STREET MARKETS

Fashion

To buy international high fashion, explore Harvey Nichols (▶ 71) and the stores lining Sloane Street, Brompton Cross, Beauchamp Place, Bond Street, South Molton Street, and St. Christopher's Place. For more dramatic, innovative, streetwise fashion, explore Hyper-Hyper and Kensington Market (both ✉ Kensington High Street, W8), then visit Vivienne Westwood (✉ 6 Davies Street, W1), American Retro (✉ 35 Old Compton Street, W1) and, in Covent Garden, Michiko Koshino (✉ 70 Neal Street, WC2), Jones (✉ 13 Floral Street, WC2), Space NK (✉ 41 Earlham Street, WC2), Sign of the Times (✉ Shorts Gardens, WC2), and Red or Dead (✉ 33 Neal Street, WC2).

Smithfield meat market

Smithfields (EC1) is the only large, fresh-food, commercial market left in Central London. Thousands of bloody carcasses hung up on iron hooks are traded in Horace Jones's grand 19th-century building. Trading starts at 5AM and the market closes down at noon (Mon–Fri).

BERMONDSEY MARKET (NEW CALEDONIAN MARKET)

You need to know your stuff here. And as the big dealers and auction-house experts get here before dawn, the earlier you go the better.

✚ L7 ✉ Long Lane and Bermondsey Street, SE1 🕐 Fri 5–2 🚇 Borough or London Bridge

BRIXTON MARKET

Best to go on Saturday, when the streets buzz with local African and Caribbean community shoppers buying their mangoes, sweet potatoes, snapper fish, calf's feet, and ready-cooked delicacies.

✉ Brixton Station Road, Electric Avenue and Popes Road, SW9 🕐 Mon–Wed, Fri–Sat 8–6; Thu 8–1 🚇 Brixton 🚃 Brixton

CAMDEN MARKETS

The small, vibrant market in Camden Lock has expanded and spawned other markets to fill every patch of space from the Underground station up to Hawley Road. Find crafts, clothes, books, etc.

✚ E2 ✉ Camden High Street to Chalk Farm Road, NW1 🕐 Sat, Sun 8–6 🚇 Camden Town

CAMDEN PASSAGE

Bargain hard at the large, twice-weekly open-air antiques market held in front of the antiques stores; then try Chapel Street general market across Upper Street.

✚ H3 ✉ Islington, N1 🕐 Wed 9–mid-afternoon, Sat 9–5 🚇 Angel

GREENWICH MARKET

Hundreds of stalls selling antiques and crafts, clothes, old books and more. A good start to a Greenwich day (▶ 20).

✉ College Approach, Stockwell Street and corner of High Road and Royal Hill, SE10 🕐 Sat–Sun 9–6 🚇 Greenwich or Island Gardens DLR then walk through the tunnel

LEADENHALL MARKET

A surprising City treat housed under Horace Jones's 1880s arcades, with quality butchers, cheesemongers, fish-mongers, etc., plus pubs.

✚ K5 ✉ Leadenhall, EC3 🕐 Mon–Fri 8–4 🚇 Bank or Monument

PETTICOAT LANE MARKET

Originally a Tudor clothes market; Jewish immigration stimulated its growth into Victorian London's largest market; bargain hard for fashion, leather, household goods, and knickknacks. Brick Lane market is near by.

✚ K5 ✉ Middlesex Street, E1 🕐 Sun 9–2 🚇 Aldgate or Aldgate East

PORTOBELLO MARKET

Saturday is the big day, when antiques and not-so-antiques are sold from the stores and the solid line of stalls in front of them. There are lower prices lower down the hill, with second-hand stalls beneath Westway.

✚ B5 ✉ Portobello Road, W11 🕐 Fruit and vegetables: Mon–Sat. General: Fri 8–3. Antiques: Sat 8–5 🚇 Ladbroke Grove

MUSEUM & GALLERY SHOPS

BRITISH MUSEUM & BRITISH LIBRARY (➤ 43)

There are currently three stores, all in or around the entrance hall, plus a children's store in the first-floor Egyptian galleries; reproductions, own-brand publications and goods, excellent children's projects.

DESIGN MUSEUM (➤ 50)

Extensive and immensely chic designer goods, some with high price tags.

LONDON AQUARIUM (➤ 51)

The world beneath the seas packaged to delight and educate.

MUSEUM OF LONDON (➤ 47)

Good for souvenirs and books about London.

NATURAL HISTORY MUSEUM (➤ 26)

Thousands of dinosaurs to read about, cut out or put on the mantelpiece; plus plenty about the world since then.

NATIONAL GALLERY (➤ 39)

Two large shops, particularly good for paper goods and diaries.

NATIONAL PORTRAIT GALLERY (➤ 38)

Surprisingly large store, well stocked with books on historical figures and British history; own-brand children's book projects.

POLLOCK TOY MUSEUM (➤ 59)

Cramped, but like an Aladdin's cave for children; toys of all prices including Pollock's toy theaters.

QUEEN'S GALLERY & ROYAL MEWS (➤ 32)

The largest selection of publications and memorabilia about (and in a few instances by) the British royal family.

ROYAL ACADEMY (➤ 51)

If you cannot own a work by a Royal Academician, then buy a plate, mug, pen or book specially designed by one for the R.A. store.

ROYAL BOTANICAL GARDENS, KEW (➤ 24)

Large selection of goods and publications, many lavishly illustrated, to keep the most ardent gardener happy.

SCIENCE MUSEUM (➤ 27)

Plenty of books and projects for budding scientists of all ages.

TATE GALLERY (➤ 34)

The annual Tate diary, its pages scattered with reproductions from the Modern and British collections, is a collector's item; also an extensive collection of quality posters.

VICTORIA & ALBERT MUSEUM (➤ 28)

You could do a full-scale Christmas shop here, from toys and books to unique crafts; many collection-inspired goods.

Specialty shops

Specialty shops come in every shape and size. Stanley Gibbons (✉ 399 Strand, WC2) is a philatelist's paradise, while James Smith & Sons (✉ 53 New Oxford Street, W1) stocks every kind of umbrella to keep British rain at bay. Other favorites include Christopher Farr (✉ 115 Regents Park Road, NW1) for contemporary carpets, the Crafts Council Shop (✉ 44 Pentonville Road, N1 and at the V&A ➤ 28), Creativity (✉ 45 New Oxford Street, WC1) for needlework materials, Paperchase (✉ 213 Tottenham Court Road, W1) and Smythson's (✉ 44 New Bond Street, W1), both stationers. To find the specialty shop you want, use the Yellow Pages telephone directory, which is listed by subject.

75

BOOKS, NEW & OLD

Electronic bargains

To Europeans, London prices for electrical goods seem cheap; to Americans they seem expensive. If you know what you want, compare prices up and down Tottenham Court Road for stereos, and look there and also in New Oxford Street for computers. Micro Anvika, on Tottenham Court Road, is good for hardware, software and CD-ROMs. If daunted, go to Selfridges or Harrods (➤ 71).

THE ATRIUM BOOKSHOP
International books and catalogues on the fine and applied arts; especially strong on current exhibitions. Good customer service, and can obtain any art book or pamphlet if it is in print.
➕ F5 ✉ 5 Cork Street, W1 ☎ 0171 495 0073 Ⓖ Green Park or Piccadilly

BERNARD QUARITCH
It is best to make an appointment to come to this, the most splendid and serious of the city's antiquarian bookstores.
➕ F5 ✉ 5 Lower John Street, W1 ☎ 0171 734 2983 Ⓖ Piccadilly Circus

BOOKS FOR COOKS
Possibly the world's best selection of books about cooking and cuisine; orders are taken and dispatched worldwide.
➕ A5 ✉ 4 Blenheim Crescent, W11 ☎ 0171 221 1992 Ⓖ Ladbroke Grove

DAUNT BOOKS FOR TRAVELLERS
In his paneled and stained-glass elegant 1910 shop, James Daunt keeps an impressive stock of travelogues and guides.
➕ E4 ✉ 83 Marylebone High Street, NW1 ☎ 0171 224 2295 Ⓖ Baker Street

DILLONS
This is now London's most extensive bookstore; good search service; many smaller branches around the capital. It sells access to the Internet.
➕ F4 ✉ 82 Gower Street, WC1 ☎ 0171 636 1577 Ⓖ Goodge Street

FORBIDDEN PLANET
An amazing selection of fantasy, horror, science fiction, and comic books of all kinds.
➕ G5 ✉ 71–73 New Oxford Street, W1 ☎ 0171 836 4179 Ⓖ Tottenham Court Road

HATCHARDS
Opened in 1797; past patrons have included Wellington and Gladstone. Hatchards still knows how to make book-buying a delicious experience, with well-informed staff.
➕ F6 ✉ 187 Piccadilly, W1 ☎ 0171 493 9921 Ⓖ Piccadilly Circus

MAGGS BROTHERS
Make your appointment, then step into this Mayfair mansion to find an out-of-print book, a first edition or rare antiquarian book.
➕ E6 ✉ 50 Berkeley Square, W1 ☎ 0171 493 7160 Ⓖ Green Park

STANFORD'S
London's largest selection of maps of countries, cities, and even very small towns around the world, together with travel books.
➕ G5 ✉ 12–14 Long Acre, WC2 ☎ 0171 836 1321 Ⓖ Covent Garden

ZWEMMER
Art books fill three neighboring bookstores, divided by category. Here, fine art is upstairs, decorative art and architecture downstairs. Photography and media at 80 Charing Cross Road; East European titles at 28 Denmark Street.
➕ G5 ✉ 24 Litchfield Street, WC2 ☎ 0171 240 4158 Ⓖ Leicester Square

FOOD & WINE

With so many parks and benches to choose from in London, a picnic makes a good break from a hard morning's sightseeing or shopping. The big stores have some of the most seductive food halls—and they stock wine; see Harrods (▶ 71), Selfridges (▶ 71), Fortnum & Mason (▶ 71) and Marks & Spencer (▶ 71). Old Compton Street (▶ 70) is a food shopper's delight; see also Clarke's (▶ 70) and cafés (▶ 70), that sell their own prepared food to take away.

BERRY BROS & RUDD
Opened as a grocery store in 1699; the wines here range from popular varietals to specialty madeiras, ports, and clarets. Their own-label bottles are always good value; perfect service.
🔢 F6 ✉ 3 St. James's Street, SW1 ☎ 0171 396 9600
🚇 Green Park

THE BLOOMSBURY WINE AND SPIRIT COMPANY
In addition to wines, the strength of this store is its Scottish malt whiskys: there are more than 170 in stock.
🔢 G4 ✉ 3 Bloomsbury Street, WC1 ☎ 0171 436 4763/4
🚇 Tottenham Court Road

CARLUCCIO'S
A designer deli, stocking only the most refined goods, such as truffle oil, black pasta, and balsamic vinegar.
🔢 G5 ✉ 30 Neal Street, WC2 ☎ 0171 240 1487 🚇 Covent Garden

FRATELLI CAMISA
This Charlotte Street store is one of London's best-loved Italian delicatessens.
🔢 F5 ✉ 53 Charlotte Street, W1 ☎ 0171 255 1240
🚇 Goodge Street

NEAL'S YARD DAIRY
A temple to the British cheese, where more than 50 varieties from small farms around Britain are ripened to perfection.
🔢 G5 ✉ 17 Shorts Gardens, WC2 ☎ 0171 379 7646
🚇 Covent Garden

ODDBINS
With more than 60 branches in London, Oddbins is strong on quality, range and price.
🔢 G5 ✉ 23 Earlham Street, WC2 ☎ 0171 836 6331
🚇 Covent Garden

VILLANDRY
If the few tables at the back of the store are all taken, then buy bread, oil, quiches and pies and make your way to Regent's Park.
🔢 E4 ✉ 89 Marylebone High Street, W1 ☎ 0171 224 3799
🚇 Baker Street or Regent's Park

WILD OATS
Five hundred customers a day explore the three floors of good-quality whole and organic food.
🔢 B5 ✉ 210 Westbourne Grove, W11 ☎ 0171 229 1063
🚇 Notting Hill Gate or Westbourne Park

Wine
London has an unrivalled variety of international wines at the best prices, for, although Britain is not a major wine-producing country, the British like to drink wine and know about it. This explains the range, quality, and fiercely competitive prices in the chains (Oddbins, Threshers) and the supermarkets (Sainsbury's, Waitrose, and Tesco). For bulk buying, consider the Majestic Warehouse chain, a reliable wine merchant, or Christie's and Sotheby's regular wine auctions (▶ 72).

THEATER

Theater tips

If you care about where you sit, go in person and peruse the plan. For an evening "Sold out" performance, it is worth lining up for returns; otherwise, try for a matinee. The cheapest seats could be far from the stage or uncomfortable, so take binoculars and a cushion. As for dress, Londoners rarely dress up for the theater any more; but they do order their intermission drinks before the play starts, and remain seated while they applaud.

Cheap ticket tips

Use the SOLT Half-price Ticket Booth. Preview tickets are cheaper, as are matinee tickets. Get up early and line up for one-day cheap tickets at the RNT. Go with friends and make a party booking at a reduced rate. Ask the National Theatre, RSC, Royal Court and other theaters about cheap tickets; and keep student and senior citizen cards at the ready. Remember, the show is the same wherever you sit!

Theater in London covers a wide range of venues. It is vibrant, varied, and extensive. The following is intended to help theater-goers find the experience they want.

INFORMATION

Time Out, London's weekly entertainment guide, provides an exhaustive list of all theaters, plus reviews. Daily newspapers carry a less complete but totally up-to-date listing, with more reviews. Ticket prices are cheap for fringe, more expensive for West End and very expensive for musicals.

TICKET BUYING

Telephone booking can be done using a credit card, which must be produced when collecting the tickets. If you book without a credit card, you must usually arrive at the theater 40 minutes before curtain-up—or else the tickets will be resold. Booking in person means you can see the seating plan, a good idea if you want a decent seat in some of London's older theaters; ask for information on leg room and sightlines.

TICKET AGENCIES

Ticketmaster (☎ 0171 344 4444) and First Call (☎ 0171 420 0000) are both reliable. Some shows have no booking fee, others a small one, and a few rise to 22 percent of ticket price, so ask first. Beware: it is unwise to buy from small agencies, and very unwise to buy from scalpers.

SOLT HALF-PRICE TICKET BOOTH

Each day a limited number of tickets for some West End shows is sold for that day's performance at half price, plus a £2 service charge. The rules are: no credit cards; a maximum of four tickets per person, no exchanges or returns. 🚻 65 ✉ Leicester Square, WC2 🕐 Mon–Sat 1–6:30; matinee days noon–6:30 🚇 Leicester Square or Piccadilly Circus

THE THEATER YEAR

The theaters are never dark. At any one time there will be an average of 45 West End theaters playing a range of musicals, drama, comedy and thrillers, as well as staging opera and dance. For festivals, many with theatrical events, ► 22. LIFT (the London International Festival of Theater) takes place in July and August in alternate years. The Royal Shakespeare Company holds an annual festival, often at the Almeida theater.

WEST END THEATERS

The Society of London Theatres (SOLT) represents the owners, managers, and producers of 54 major London theaters. SOLT runs the annual Lawrence Olivier Awards, London's answer to the Tonys, publishes the fortnightly London Theater Guide (free from theaters) and runs a Theater Token scheme (☎ 0171 240 8800) and the SOLT Half-price Ticket Booth (see above).

ROYAL NATIONAL THEATRE (RNT)

British and world drama, classics and new plays. Home of the National Theatre company, it has three performance spaces —the Olivier, the Lyttelton and the Cottesloe. All have several productions in repertory.

🏠 H6 ✉ South Bank , SE1 ☎ Information and tours: 0171 633 0880. Theater tickets: 0171 928 2252 🚇 Embankment or Waterloo 🚆 Waterloo

ROYAL SHAKESPEARE THEATRE (RSC)

The London home of the Royal Shakespeare Company, who perform in season in the Barbican Theatre (level 3) and The Pit (level 1). Some productions are new, others are from Stratford; several productions may be running concurrently in repertory. There is an annual Prom season, plus backstage tours.

🏠 J4 ✉ Barbican Centre, Silk Street, EC2 ☎ 0171 638 4141. Recorded information: 0171 628 2295. Booking: 0171 638 8891. Range of cheap ticket deals 🚇 Barbican

MUSICALS

The successful, long-running shows are dominated by the great impresarios. Sir Andrew Lloyd Webber, who restored and owns the Palace Theatre, has staged *Starlight Express*, *Sunset Boulevard*, *Phantom of the Opera* and *Cats*, the latter two with Cameron Mackintosh, who has had great success with his *Les Misérables*.

LONG-RUNNING STALWARTS

Few plays have the sustained, long-running success of the musicals. Most famous is Agatha Christie's *The Mousetrap* at St. Martin's, aiming for its 50th anniversary in 2002. At the Fortune Theatre, *The Woman in Black* began its run in 1989.

OFF–WEST END THEATER

This new category honors the fringe theaters that still stage imaginative productions. Look in the listings for the Almeida, the Bush, Donmar Warehouse, Drill Hall, the Gate, Hampstead, ICA, King's Head, Lyric Studio, Riverside Studios, Royal Court, Theatre Royal Stratford East, Tricycle, the Young Vic.

FRINGE AND PUB-THEATER

True fringe, or "alternative" theater in London is vibrant, varied, and dotted about in over 35 venues, many of them pubs. Try Etcetera Theatre (at the Oxford Arms pub), Finborough, the Hen & Chickens, Man in the Moon, New End Theatre, Old Red Lion, and the White Bear.

COMEDY

The Comedy Store is hugely popular. Also try the Hurricane Club, Banana Cabaret, Jongleurs at the Cornet, Comedy Café, Red Rose Cabaret, and Hackney Empire, a restored music hall that holds vaudeville nights.

Open-air theater

If the weather is good, grab a picnic and head for the Open-Air Theatre, Regent's Park (Jun–Sep), Greenwich Old Observatory (Jul–Aug) or Holland Park Theatre (Jun–Aug).

Children's theater

Several theaters stage magical performances year-round. Names to look for include the Little Angel Marionette Theatre (doyenne of puppet theaters), Polka Children's Theatre and the Unicorn Theatre for Children. Watch for children's productions at the National and the RSC, as well as Punch and Judy shows in Covent Garden Piazza.

Revived theaters

Some old London theaters have been revived. Andrew Lloyd Webber restored his 1880s Cambridge Theatre. The Theatre Royal, Haymarket, has new gold leaf, while the Savoy and the Criterion have been meticulously restored. Out of the West End, the Richmond Theatre has reopened, and Islington's Collins Music Hall will do so in 1999. On the south bank, Sir Peter Hall's company is in the revived Old Vic Theatre and a smallscale Globe Theatre opened in 1997, designed in the manner of Burbage's original where Shapeskeare worked.

CLASSICAL MUSIC, OPERA & BALLET

Food with music

The choice is wide (see Jazz, ► 81). For starters, there are tea dances at the Waldorf Hotel (► 64). Claridges' cocktails with their Hungarian Quartet are an institution, while a dinner-dance at the Savoy, Ritz and Claridges is opulently romantic (► 84). Smollensky's (► 62), Rock Garden (✉ 5–6 The Piazza, Covent Garden, WC2), Deals West (✉ 14–16 Foubert's Place, W1), Break for the Border (✉ 8 Argyll Street, W1) and Pizza Pomodoro (✉ 51 Beauchamp Place, SW3) are altogether more informal. But if the weather is good, do as Londoners do and head for a park (see Music everywhere!, opposite).

Glyndebourne

Glyndebourne Festival Opera (late May–Aug) is only a train ride away in Sussex. Performances begin late afternoon, with long intervals for picnics in the sumptuous grounds. It makes a delightful outing, and the train service is good. ✉ Glyndebourne, Lewes, Sussex BN8 5UU ☎ 01273 813813

THE MUSIC YEAR

Runs non-stop. Look for festivals such as the City of London, Spitalfields, Almeida and Hampton Court Palace , and traditions such as the Christmas Oratorios, carol singing in Trafalgar Square and the Easter Passions. The major classic festival is the Proms, a nickname for the Henry Wood Promenade Concerts, held daily at the Royal Albert Hall and elsewhere from mid-July to mid-September, and broadcast live on B.B.C. Radio 3.

THE DANCE YEAR

Very lively, with great variety. Highpoints include the Coliseum's summer season, the Royal Ballet's performances at the Royal Opera House and the Nutcracker Suite season at the Royal Festival Hall (Dec–Jan). Other major venues are: Sadler's Wells, the Place, I.C.A., and Riverside Studios. The climax of the year is Dance Umbrella, a world showcase for contemporary dance (Oct–Nov).

THE OPERA YEAR

Grand opera alternates with dance at the Royal Opera House. Cheaper and often more vibrant opera takes place at the larger Coliseum (performances in English). In addition, there are visits from Welsh National Opera, Opera North and Opera Factory, and open-air opera performances in Holland Park and by Kenwood Lake.

MAJOR VENUES

BARBICAN CONCERT HALL
✚ J4 ✉ Barbican Centre, Silk Street, EC2 ☎ 0171 638 4141. Recorded information: 0171 628 2295. Booking: 0171 638 8891. Credit card booking: daily 9–8, 0171 638 8891. Range of cheap ticket deals 🚇 Barbican

LONDON COLISEUM
✚ G5 ✉ St. Martin's Lane, WC2 ☎ 0171 632 8300 🚇 Leicester Square

ROYAL ALBERT HALL
✚ C6 ✉ Kensington Gore, SW7 ☎ Information: 0171 589 3203. Booking: 0171 589 8212 🚇 South Kensington

ROYAL OPERA HOUSE
Undergoing alterations. Alternative venues. ✚ G5 ✉ Covent Garden, WC2 ☎ 0171 304 4000 🚇 Covent Garden

SADLER'S WELLS THEATRE
The rebuilt theater opens late 1998. Meanwhile, find the Company at the Peacock Theatre, Kingsway, WC2 (☎ 0171 314 9002). ✚ H3 ✉ Rosebery Avenue, EC1 ☎ 0171 312 1996 🚇 Angel

SOUTH BANK
Royal Festival Hall, Queen Elizabeth Hall and Purcell Room. ✚ G6–H6 ✉ South Bank, SE1 ☎ Recorded information: 0171 633 0932. Booking: 0171 960 9242 🚇 Waterloo

WIGMORE HALL
✚ E5 ✉ 36 Wigmore Street, W1 ☎ 0171 935 2141 🚇 Bond Street

JAZZ & PUB MUSIC

London boasts a great concentration of world-class jazz musicians, both home-grown and foreign, traditional and contemporary; look out for Camden Jazz Week, Capital Jazz Festival and the Bracknell Festival. The city also vibrates with evening and late-night gigs covering rock, roots, R&B and much more, some found in pubs. For a full list of venues, check in *Time Out*.

BULL'S HEAD, BARNES
Seductive combination of good jazz in the friendly village atmosphere of a riverside pub.
➕ Off map at A10 ✉ 373 Lonsdale Road, SW13 ☎ 0181 876 5241

DOVER STREET WINE BAR
Large, candle-lit, popular basement where the music can be jump-jive, jazz, R&B or Big Band and where the food is good.
➕ F6 ✉ 8–9 Dover Street, W1 ☎ 0171 629 9813 🚇 Piccadilly Circus

DUBLIN CASTLE
Friendly pub for enjoying a variety of folk, rock 'n' roll, blues and soul.
➕ F2 ✉ 94 Parkway, NW1 ☎ 0171 485 1773 🚇 Camden Town

HALF MOON PUTNEY
Jolly pub for R&B played by lesser stars; plenty of audience participation.
➕ Off map at A10 ✉ 93 Lower Richmond Road, SW15 ☎ 0181 780 9383

JAZZ CAFÉ
Current favorite among the young; buzzes nightly with the widest range of jazz, from soul to rap.
➕ F2 ✉ 5 Parkway, NW1 ☎ 0171 344 0044 🚇 Camden Town

MEAN FIDDLER
Pub popular for its beer and wide variety of music, which is played in the main hall and the smaller acoustic room.
➕ Off map at A1 ✉ 22–28a High Street, Harlesden, NW10 ☎ 0181 963 0940

PIZZA EXPRESS, SOHO
Quality pizzas and great, often mainstream, jazz in this friendly Soho cellar. Several other branches of Pizza Express have live jazz, too.
➕ F5 ✉ 10 Dean Street, W1 ☎ 0171 439 8722 🚇 Tottenham Court Road

PIZZA ON THE PARK
More upscale than its sister, Pizza Express; top foreign names play at one or other venue.
➕ E6 ✉ 11 Knightsbridge, SW1 ☎ 0171 235 5273 🚇 Hyde Park Corner

RONNIE SCOTT'S
One of the world's best-known and most loved jazz clubs, run by jazz musicians for jazz lovers.
➕ F5 ✉ 47 Frith Street, W1 ☎ 0171 439 0747 🚇 Tottenham Court Road

STATION TAVERN
Notting Hill pub that is London's hub for all blues acoustic, R&B and folk.
✉ 41 Bramley Road, W10 ☎ 0171 727 4053 🚇 Ladbroke Grove

Pub music
This can be one of the cheapest and most enjoyable evenings out in London, worth the trip to an off-beat location. For the price of a pint of beer (usually a huge choice) you can settle down to enjoy the ambience and listen to some of the best alternative music available in town, from folk, jazz, and blues to R&B, soul, and more. Audiences tend to be friendly, loyal to their venue, and happy to talk music.

Music everywhere!
London is full of music. At lunchtime, the best places are churches, where the regular concerts are usually free. Look in *Time Out* listings (➤ 79) for: in the City, St. Anne and St. Agnes, St. Olave's; in the West End, St. James's, Piccadilly. St Paul's Cathedral Evensong is mid-afternoon. On Sundays, cathedrals and churches are again best for sacred music. Look for concerts in historic houses, museums and galleries, especially during the City of London Festival (July). Finally, music is played outdoors in the royal parks, Embankment Gardens, and elsewhere, but best of all at Kenwood (➤ 29) or Marble Hill, Richmond, on summer evenings.

MOVIES & CLUBS

London lacks the range of movie theaters to be found in some other cities and often receives foreign films long after their home release. But there is plenty of independent and late-night cinema, making a good beginning to a night of clubbing. Some cinema seats are half-price on Mondays.

One-night clubbing is strong. To find the right club night and club style, consult *Time Out*'s night-by-night listing (➤ 78 and 79) or see the advertisements at regular venues. Dress streetwise and pay at the door.

Cocktails and bars

Apart from a handful, including Smollensky's-on-the-Strand (➤ 62) and Mezzo (➤ 65), the best bars are in hotels. For plushness, the Lanesborough (✉ Hyde Park Corner, SW1) and Langham (✉ Langham Place, SW1) are best. For pampering, head for the Savoy's Thames Foyer and Claridge's lounge (➤ 84). For New York style try the Savoy's American Bar (➤ 84). To be seen, go to the Dorchester (✉ Park Lane, W1). To be discreet, go to the Connaught (➤ 69). London's best private bar is at Morton's, a club in Berkeley Square club that offers temporary membership.

CINEMAS

THE BIG SCREENS

The places to see commercial first runs, but prices are high. Biggest screens are Empire, Leicester Square (Cinema 1), and Odeon, Leicester Square. Beware of old cinemas divided into multi-screen complexes.

THE INDEPENDENTS

Show a mixture of commercial first runs, foreign (subtitled) and off-beat British films. The most sumptuous are the Minema, Lumière, Curzon Mayfair, Barbican, and the Chelsea Cinema; others include the Screen chain, Camden Plaza, Gate, Metro, and Renoir.

NATIONAL FILM THEATRE

Located next to the Museum of the Moving Image, with two cinemas. Its advantages: good programing, silent audiences, film-buff bookstore, riverside restaurant, children's screenings.
🚇 H6 ✉ South Bank, SE1 ☎ 0171 928 3232 🚇 Waterloo

REPERTORY

Good for old movies, seasons, double-bills and late nights. Try the Everyman and the Phoenix; knife-edge contemporary at ICA Cinémathèque; variety at the French and Goethe Institutes. Also go to the Museum of London's "Made in London" series (➤ 47).

CLUBS

BORDERLINE

Mill with the music business insiders.
🚇 G5 ✉ Orange Yard, off Manette Street, W1 ☎ 0171 734 2095 🚇 Tottenham Court Road

BRIXTON ACADEMY

Splendid building; best on Friday and Saturday.
🚇 Off map at H10 ✉ 211 Stockwell Road, SW9 ☎ 0171 924 9999 🚇 Stockwell

CAMDEN PALACE

Friendly ambience for a bargain night out; indie bands on Tuesdays.
🚇 F2 ✉ 1a Camden High Street, NW1 ☎ 0171 387 0428 🚇 Camden Town

EQUINOX DISCOTHEQUE, EMPIRE BALLROOM

The best for an energetic bop on a crowded floor.
🚇 G5 ✉ Leicester Square, WC2 ☎ 0171 437 1446 🚇 Leicester Square

THE GARDENING CLUB

Covent Garden's busiest club.
🚇 G5 ✉ 4 The Piazza, WC2 ☎ 0171 497 3154 🚇 Covent Garden

GOSSIPS

Young and friendly, with varied theme nights.
🚇 F5 ✉ 69 Dean Street, W1 ☎ 0171 434 4480 🚇 Tottenham Court Road

THE VENUE

Worth the journey to hear the best indie bands.
🚇 N9 ✉ 2a Clifton Rise, New Cross, SE14 ☎ 0181 692 4077 🚇 New Cross or New Cross Gate

SPECTATOR SPORTS

You can watch and play most sports either in or near London (often merely an Underground ride away). Major events are held on Saturdays and Sundays; tickets are readily available (see ticket agencies ➤ 78–79).

THE MAJOR VENUES

ALL ENGLAND LAWN TENNIS CHAMPIONSHIPS, WIMBLEDON

Tennis's top tournament starts late June. Enter the ticket ballot or join lines for ticket, except on the last four days.
✉ All England Lawn Tennis and Croquet Club, Church Road, SW19 ☎ 0181 946 2244 Ⓔ Southfields

CRYSTAL PALACE NATIONAL SPORTS CENTRE

The major venue for national competitions.
✉ Ledrington Road SE19 ☎ 0181 778 0131 Ⓔ Crystal Palace

LORD'S CRICKET GROUND

Home of the MCC (Marylebone Cricket Club ➤ 60); watch Middlesex play home games, test cricket, major finals and Sunday league games.
➕ D3 ✉ St. John's Wood Road, NW8 ☎ 0171 289 8979 Ⓔ St John's Wood

THE OVAL

Surrey home games and test cricket; also Sunday league games.
➕ H8 ✉ Surrey County Cricket Club, The Oval, SE11 ☎ 0171 582 6660 Ⓔ Oval

ROYAL ALBERT HALL

Grand Victorian building holding 5,000 spectators; boxing, tennis and sumo-wrestling events.
➕ C6 ✉ Kensington Gore, SW7 ☎ 0171 589 8212 Ⓔ South Kensington

WEMBLEY STADIUM AND ARENA

A vast complex with Stadium, Arena and Conference and Exhibition Centre. Excellent visitors' tours of the Stadium.
✉ Wembley, Middlesex ☎ 0181 900 1234. Tours: 0181 902 8833 Ⓔ Wembley Park

OTHER MAJOR SPORTS

ASSOCIATION FOOTBALL (SOCCER)

To see the FA Cup final (May) at Wembley, pay high prices; alternatively, visit one of the 12 London clubs (Aug–May) such as Arsenal, Chelsea, Fulham, or Tottenham Hotspur.

AUTO RACING

Plenty of action at Brands Hatch in Kent: racing most weekends of the year, usually motorbikes on Saturdays, cars on Sundays.

RUGBY UNION

Tickets for the internationals at Twickenham are scarce; it is easier to watch the Varsity match (Dec), the Cup Final (Apr–May) or take in a tour game, and easier still to watch a game at one of the ten London clubs such as Blackheath or Harlequins.

Participatory sports

London's many parks and open spaces are alive with people playing tennis, bowls, cricket and soccer, or jogging, walking, and boating. For more formal sports, Crystal Palace National Sports Centre has comprehensive facilities; but Kensington Sports Centre (✉ Walmer Road, W1), the Oasis (✉ 32 Endell Street, WC2), and the Queen Mother Sports Centre (✉ 223 Vauxhall Bridge Road, SW1) are more central. Barbican Health & Fitness Centre and Broadgate Club (at the Broadgate Centre, ➤ 54) have good fitness equipment.

Horse-racing

A British obsession, so there are plenty of races near London during the flat season (Mar–Nov) and winter steeple-chasing (Aug–May). On and off course, betting is legal and well governed. Daytime races at Newmarket, Epsom, Goodwood and Ascot can be reached by train from London, or take the train out to Windsor or Kempton for a delightful summer evening meeting. Daily newspapers have details of race meetings.

83

LUXURY HOTELS

To be pampered amid sumptuous surroundings may be an essential part of your vacation. London's most luxurious hotels have been built with no expense spared. A single room costs from £210 per night, sometimes considerably more.

Bargain deals

London hotel prices are very high. But quality rooms can be had for bargain prices. Most deluxe and middle-market hotels offer weekend deals throughout the year, to include breakfast, dinner and even theater tickets. The big chains such as Forte, Mount Charlotte Thistle, and Best Western have brochures offering package deals. Newly refurbished hotels usually have incentive prices, and off-season months such as January and February are a buyer's market.

CLARIDGE'S
From the art deco lobby and mirrored dining room to the huge baths and log fires in the corner suites, this is deluxe Mayfair living.
➕ E5 ✉ Brook Street, W1 ☎ 0171 629 8860; fax 0171 499 2210 Ⓜ Bond Street

DUKES
A stone's throw from St. James's Palace, the aristocratic and intimate flavor of an old St. James's mansion is enhanced by the discreet dining rooms reserved for guests.
➕ F6 ✉ 35 St. James's Place, SW1 ☎ 0171 491 4840; fax 0171 493 1264 Ⓜ Green Park

FOUR SEASONS HOTEL
Formerly called Inn on the Park, this modern hotel may lack period style, but it provides some of the best service in town.
➕ E6 ✉ Hamilton Place, Park Lane, W1 ☎ 0171 499 0888; fax 0171 493 6629 Ⓜ Hyde Park Corner

HALKIN HOTEL
Central London's first deluxe hotel built and furnished in contemporary design throughout, with a suitably upscale Italian restaurant. An ideal location for visits to Knightsbridge and Mayfair.
➕ E6 ✉ 4 Halkin Street, SW1 ☎ 0171 333 1000; fax 0171 333 1100 Ⓜ Hyde Park Corner

HYATT CARLTON TOWER
Modern yet opulent, from the lobby flower arrangements to the rooftop health club.
➕ E7 ✉ 2 Cadogan Place, SW1 ☎ 0171 235 1234; fax 0171 235 9129 Ⓜ Knightsbridge

MERIDIEN PICCADILLY
Residents can use Champneys health club, which fills the basement; French influence in the well-appointed rooms.
➕ F6 ✉ 21 Piccadilly, W1 ☎ 0171 734 8000; fax 0171 437 3574 Ⓜ Piccadilly Circus

THE RITZ
Small but sumptuous, with plenty of old style, gilt decor and the great first-floor promenade to London's most beautiful dining room, overlooking Green Park.
➕ F6 ✉ Piccadilly W1 ☎ 0171 493 8181; fax 0171 493 2687 Ⓜ Green Park

SAVOY
Old-style Thameside hotel between the West End and the City; splendid river suites; art deco rooms; health club.
➕ G5 ✉ Strand, WC2 ☎ 0171 836 4343; fax 0171 872 8901 Ⓜ Aldwych or Embankment

THE STAFFORD
Tucked behind Piccadilly, with an alley through to Green Park, this small, discreet hotel has a similar intimacy to Dukes but its cozy public rooms are open to non-guests.
➕ F6 ✉ 16 St. James's Place, SW1 ☎ 0171 493 0111; fax 0171 493 7121 Ⓜ Green Park

MID-RANGE HOTELS

BASIL STREET HOTEL

Tucked behind Harrods and full of old-style comforts, favored by discerning Americans.

✚ D7 ✉ Basil Street, SW3 ☎ 0171 581 3311; fax 0171 581 3693 🚇 Knightsbridge

5 SUMNER PLACE HOTEL

Family-run house-hotel, in chic South Kensington residential area; a dozen rooms, and a garden.

✚ C7 ✉ 5 Sumner Place, SW7 ☎ 0171 584 7586; fax 0171 823 9962 🚇 South Kensington

HAZLITT'S

Right in the heart of Soho; residents in this period house can stroll to the major galleries and museums in minutes.

✚ F5 ✉ 6 Frith Street, Soho Square, W1 ☎ 0171 434 1771; fax 0171 439 1524 🚇 Tottenham Court Road

HOLIDAY INN VICTORIA

This consistently reliable chain has a clutch of central London hotels. Find them at Oxford Circus, Kensington, Mayfair and King's Cross.

✚ F7 ✉ 2 Bridge Place, Victoria, SW1 ☎ 0171 834 8123; fax 0171 828 1099 🚇 Victoria

HOTEL NUMBER SIXTEEN

Long-established champion of the many delightful London house-hotels (converted from four Victorian houses); log fires, walled garden.

✚ C7 ✉ 16 Sumner Place, SW7 ☎ 0171-589 5232; fax 0171-584 8615 🚇 South Kensington

MONTAGUE PARK HOTEL

Bloomsbury houses converted into a traditional hotel; terrace and garden.

✚ G4 ✉ 12–20 Montague Street, WC1 ☎ 0171 637 1001; fax 0171 637 2516 🚇 Holborn or Russell Square

REMBRANDT

Large Edwardian hotel ideal for Knightsbridge and South Kensington, with a health club.

✚ D7 ✉ 11 Thurloe Place, SW7 ☎ 0171 589 8100; fax 0171 225 3363 🚇 South Kensington

ROYAL OVER-SEAS LEAGUE

Central location; garden overlooking Green Park; no-fuss rooms and restaurant; membership open to all British and Commonwealth citizens and members of affiliated clubs worldwide.

✚ F6 ✉ Over-Seas House, Park Place, St. James's Street, SW1 ☎ 0171 408 0214; fax 0171 499 6738 🚇 Green Park

SHAFTESBURY

Small hotel in busy Soho, convenient to theatreland.

✚ F5 ✉ 65–73 Shaftesbury Avenue, W1 ☎ 0171 434 4200; fax 0171 437 1717 🚇 Piccadilly Circus

WHITEHALL HOTEL

Excellent location for Covent Garden and Soho, with a big backyard for relaxing. Rooms exceptionally well decorated and appointed.

✚ G4 ✉ 2–5 Montague Street, WC1 ☎ 0171 580 5871; fax 0171 580 5554 🚇 Holborn or Russell Square

Expect to pay between £70 and £130 per night for a single room in mid-range hotels.

Beware of hidden hotel costs

The room price quoted by a hotel may, or may not, include Continental breakfast or full English breakfast and VAT, which is currently 17.5 percent. Since these affect the final bill dramatically, it is vital to check. Also, check the percentage mark-up on telephone calls, which can be high—there may even be charges for using a telephone charge card or receiving a fax; and ask about the laundry and pressing service, which can be very slow.

BUDGET ACCOMMODATIONS

Budget accommodations can cost anywhere between £20 and £70 per night for a single room.

Location is everything

It is well worth perusing the London map to decide where you are likely to spend most of your time. Then select a hotel in that area or accessible to it by Underground on a direct line, so you avoid having to change trains. London is vast and it takes time to cross it, particularly by bus and costly taxis. By paying a little more to be in the center and near your activities, you will save on travel time and costs.

Youth hostels

There are seven hostels in Central London (by Oxford Street, in Holland Park, and by St. Paul's Cathedral, for example), so book well ahead.

✉ Youth Hostels Association, Trevelyan House, 8 St. Stephen's Hill, St. Albans, Hertfordshire AL1 2DY ☎ Information: 01727 855215; fax 01727 844126. Booking: 0171 248 6547; fax 0171 236 7681

Cheap, clean hotel rooms in central London are becoming more plentiful.

ELIZABETH HOTEL
Quiet hotel overlooking a large London square, with car-parking facilities.
➕ F7 ✉ 37 Eccleston Square, SW1 ☎ 0171 828 6812; fax 0171 828 6814 🚇 Victoria

FIELDING HOTEL
Right in Covent Garden; a favorite with publishers, writers and actors. Simple.
➕ G5 ✉ 4 Broad Court, Bow Street, WC2 ☎ 0171 836 8305; fax 0171 497 0064 🚇 Covent Garden

INTERNATIONAL STUDENTS HOUSE
Rooms and family flats, located right by Regent's Park. Reserve well ahead.
➕ F4 ✉ 229 Great Portland Street, W1 ☎ 0171 631 8300; fax 0171 631 8315 🚇 Great Portland Street or Regent's Park

LA RESERVE
Out of the center but near lots of restaurants and Chelsea Football Club; refurbished period house.
➕ B9 ✉ 422–429 Fulham Road, SW6 ☎ 0171 385 8561; fax 0171 385 7662 🚇 Parsons Green

LONDON HOMESTEAD SERVICES
To stay with a London family, try this agency: 200 homes, all within 20 minutes of Piccadilly. Minimum 3-night stay.
✉ Coombe Wood Road, Kingston-upon-Thames, Surrey KT2 7JY ☎ 0181 949 4455; fax 0181 549 5492

MANZI'S
Simple rooms above a popular fish restaurant, in an area that buzzes with life day and night.
➕ G5 ✉ 1 and 2 Leicester Street, Leicester Square, WC2 ☎ 0171 734 0224; fax 0171 437 4864 🚇 Leicester Square

SWISS HOUSE HOTEL
Comfortable little hotel in a pretty residential area of South Kensington.
➕ C8 ✉ 171 Old Brompton Road, SW5 ☎ 0171 373 2769; fax 0171 373 4983 🚇 Earl's Court or Gloucester Road

THANET HOTEL
No-fuss rooms in a brick-fronted Bloomsbury terrace, ideal for Covent Garden and the theater.
➕ G4 ✉ 8 Bedford Place, WC1 ☎ 0171 636 2869; fax 0171 323 6676 🚇 Russell Square or Holborn

UNIVERSITY WOMEN'S CLUB
Two dozen rooms in an old Mayfair house; membership open to all women graduates and similarly qualified women; friends pay a temporary membership fee.
➕ E6 ✉ 2 Audley Square, South Audley Street, W1 ☎ 0171 499 2268; fax 0171 499 7046 🚇 Hyde Park Corner

VICTORIA INN
Friendly, stucco-fronted Pimlico house with practical, no-frills rooms.
➕ F7 ✉ 65–67 Belgrave Road, SW1 ☎ 0171 834 6721; fax 0171 931 0201 🚇 Victoria

WINDERMERE HOTEL
Friendly atmosphere and elegant style.
➕ F8 ✉ 142–144 Warwick Way, SW1 ☎ 0171 834 5163; fax 0171 630 8831 🚇 Victoria

LONDON
travel facts

ARRIVING & DEPARTING

Before you go

- Check that your passport is valid for the whole length of your stay.
- Passport holders from E.U. member countries, the U.S. and some Commonwealth countries (such as Australia and Canada) do not require a visa; visitors from any other country should check.
- Write to the London Tourist Board for a free information pack: ✉ 26 Grosvenor Gardens, London, SW1.

When to go

- The tourist season is year round, and almost all attractions remain open most days of the year.
- High season is June–September: arrive with a hotel reservation and pre-booked theater seats.
- Quietest months are January and February. Tickets are easier to find Monday–Thursday throughout the year.

Climate

- Officially, London is warmish in summer and coldish in winter, without extremes.
- Officially, London's rainfall is even throughout the year, rising in September and November.
- Unofficially, London's weather is unpredictable. It may be unusually mild in winter or cold in summer, and it can rain at any time. Dress in layers, and bring a raincoat.

Arriving by air

- London has five airports:

Gatwick

- Gatwick (☎ 01293 535353, 24 hours) is 30 miles south of Hyde Park Corner.
- Two terminals, North and South, each with information desks.

- Trains leave from South Terminal: Gatwick Express to Victoria Station (30 minutes); Thameslink trains via London Bridge, Blackfriars, and City Thameslink to King's Cross Station.
- Bus services include Flightline 777, from each terminal to Victoria Coach Station (at least an hour).

Heathrow

- Heathrow is 15 miles west of Hyde Park Corner.
- Terminal 1—mostly British and Continental flights ☎ 0181 745 7702. Terminal 2—mostly Continental ☎ 0181 745 7115. Terminal 3—mostly intercontinental ☎ 0181 745 7412. Terminal 4—mostly British Airways, intercontinental, Concorde, and BA's Paris and Amsterdam flights ☎ 0181 745 4540.
- All four terminals have information desks; London Tourist Board's desk is at Terminals 1, 2, and 3 Underground station.
- Quickest way to London is by Heathrow Express to Paddington Station. Or use the Underground: there are two stations, one for Terminals 1, 2 and 3 and one for Terminal 4, on the Piccadilly line which goes direct to Central London (South Kensington 40 minutes, King's Cross 50 minutes).
- Bus services include the two Airbus routes, A1 and A2, from all terminals to several London areas.
- A taxi from the official taxi rank will cost more than £30 to central London, even outside rush hours.

London City Airport

- ☎ 0171 474 5555. Located beside the City, so use a taxi or the two Airbus shuttles—to Canary Wharf (for Docklands Light Railway, which connects to the

Underground at Bank Station) or to Liverpool Street Station (which also connects to the Underground).
• For the business traveler; check-in time 15 minutes before the flight.

London Luton
• ☎ 01582 405100. 33 miles north of Central London.
• Mainly U.K. and Continental flights.
• Luton Railway Station is on the Thameslink to King's Cross; buses go to Victoria Coach Station.

Stansted
• ☎ 01279 680500. Located 30 miles northeast of Central London.
• Mostly European flights; also transatlantic flights in summer.
• Stansted Express trains run to Liverpool Street Station (40 minutes).

Arriving by sea and train
• The quickest way to London from any port is usually by train, and the cheapest is often by bus.

Arriving via the Channel Tunnel
• Eurostar trains (☎ 01233 617575) are for foot passengers only. Best to book. Trains run between Waterloo International and Paris (3 hours) or Brussels (3 hours 15 minutes), early morning to late at night.
• Le Shuttle (☎ 0990 353535) is for vehicles only. No need to book. Three an hour between Calais and Folkestone (join the M20 to London at junction 11a), 24 hours.

Arriving by car
• Driving in London is slow, parking is expensive, and fines are high. Use public transportation.
• Check with your hotel about off-street parking.

Arriving by bus
• Victoria Coach Station
  ✉ Buckingham Palace Road, SW1
  ☎ Information: 0990 808080.
  MasterCard and Visa bookings: 0171 730 3499

Customs regulations
• No limit to goods for personal use brought by visitors from E.U. member countries.
• Limits apply for other visitors; if in doubt use the red customs channel.

Departure/airport tax
• This is currently £10 and is often included in the ticket price.

ESSENTIAL FACTS

Tourist information centers
Main centers
• 🅸 Victoria Forecourt, SW1
  🕐 Daily 8–7 (Nov–Easter Mon Sat 8–6; Sun 8:30–4). The largest center, with comprehensive London information, hotel booking service and bookstore. Free maps for roads, buses and Underground, plus events sheets.
• ✉ Heathrow Terminals 1, 2 and 3, Heathrow Airport 🕐 Daily 8–6.
• ✉ Underground Station Concourse, Heathrow Airport 🕐 Daily 6AM–11PM.
• ✉ Liverpool Street Underground Station, EC2 🕐 Mon–Fri 8–8; Sat, Sun 8:45–5:30.
• ✉ Selfridges Basement Services Arcade, 400 Oxford Street, W1 ☎ 0171 629 1234 🕐 Store hours usually 9:30–7 (Thu 9:30–8).
• ✉ Waterloo International Terminus, SE1 🕐 Daily 8:30AM–10:30PM.

Local centers
• City of London Information Centre ✉ St. Paul's Churchyard, EC4 ☎ 0171 332 1456

- ◉ Apr–Sep daily 9:30–5. Oct–Mar Mon–Fri 9:30–5; Sat 9:30–12:30. Detailed information on the City of London.
- Greenwich Tourist Information Centre ✉ 46 Greenwich Church Street, Greenwich, SE10 ☎ 0181 858 6376 ◉ Daily, usually 10:15–4:45.
- Richmond Tourist Information Centre ✉ Old Town Hall, Whittaker Avenue, Richmond, Surrey ☎ 0181 940 9125 ◉ Mon–Fri 10–6, Sat 10–5 (May–Oct, also Sun 10:15–4:15).
- Southwark Tourist Information Centre ✉ Lower Level, Cottons Centre, Middle Yard, SE1 ☎ 0171 357 9294 ◉ Mon–Fri 10–5:30; Sat–Sun 11–5.
- Twickenham Tourist Information Centre ✉ The Atrium, Civic Centre, York Street, Twickenham, Middlesex ☎ 0181 891 7272 ◉ Mon–Fri 9–5.

Visitorcall

- 24-hour recorded telephone guide (◉ 0839 123456) covering over 30 subjects. Premium rates are charged. To access specific lines directly, dial 0839 123 plus 400 (what's on this week), 401 (seasonal events), 403 (exhibitions), 407 (Sundays in London), 411 (Changing the Guard), 416 (popular West End shows), 424 (where to take children), 428 (street markets), 429 (museums), 430 (traveling in London).

Hotel reservations

- The LTB (☎ 0171 824 8844) publishes an annual hotel guide, *Where to Stay in London*, and runs a hotel booking service; credit card payment only. £5 fee.

British Tourist Authority

- British Travel Centre ✉ 12 Regent Street, Piccadilly Circus, SW1 (no ☎) ◉ Mon–Fri 9–6:30; Sat–Sun 10–4 (May–Sep Sat 10–5).
- British Tourist Authority telephone information service ☎ 0181 846 9000.

Opening hours

- Major attractions: seven days a week; some open late on Sun.
- Stores: six days a week; some open on Sun. For late-night shopping (► 70).
- Banks: Mon–Fri 9:30–5; a few remain open later or open on Sat mornings. Bureaux de change have longer opening hours (including weekends).
- Post offices: usually Mon–Fri 9–5:30; Sat 9–12:30.

National holidays

- Jan 1; Good Friday; Easter Mon; first Mon in May; last Mon in May; last Mon in Aug; Dec 25; Dec 26.
- Almost all attractions close on Christmas Day. Some stores, restaurants (particularly in hotels) and attractions remain open on other holidays.

Money

- 100 pence to £1. Coins: 1p, 2p, 5p, 10p, 20p, 50p and £1; bills: £5, £10, £20 and £50. Collectors' £2 coins can be bought at banks.
- Banks often offer a better exchange rate than *bureaux de change*. Check rates, commission, and any other charges.

Tipping

- 10 percent for restaurants, taxis, hairdressers, and other services. Look over restaurant checks to see whether or not service charge has already been added or is included.
- No tipping in theaters, cinemas, concert halls or in pubs and bars (unless there is waitress service).

Places of worship
- Almost every denomination is represented. Refer to the Yellow Pages telephone directory.

Time
- G.M.T. (Greenwich Mean Time) is standard time; B.S.T. (British Summer Time: late March–late October) is one hour ahead.

Electricity
- Standard supply is 230V, with a permitted range of 216.2–253V.
- Motor-driven equipment needs a specific frequency; in the U.K. it is 50 cycles per second (kHz).

PUBLIC TRANSPORTATION

London Transport travel information centers
- Centers sell travel passes and provide Underground and train maps, bus route maps, and information on cheap tickets.
- Open daily at these stations: Victoria, Euston, King's Cross, Liverpool Street, Oxford Circus (except Sun), Piccadilly Circus, St. James's Park (except Sun); also at each terminal at Heathrow Airport and at Heathrow Terminals 1, 2 and 3 Underground station.
- London Transport enquiries telephone service: ☎ 0171 222 1234, 24 hours; 0171 222 1200.

Travel passes
- Priced according to length of validity and how many of the six London zones it covers, a pass usually pays for itself within two or three journeys. There are three main types.
- Travelcards: valid after 9:30AM for unlimited travel by Underground, British Rail, Docklands Light Railway, and most buses; on sale at travel information centers, British Rail stations, all Underground stations, and some stores (such as newspaper shops); cover travel for one day, a week, a month or a year. Adults need a photocard (except for a one-day Travelcard), on sale at travel information centers; children aged 5–15 pay child fares but need a child-rate photocard; children under five travel free.
- Bus passes: bus-only passes are on sale at travel information centers, Underground stations, and some newspaper shops.
- Visitor Travelcards: similar to Travelcards but no need for a photo; valid for one, three, four or seven days. Must be bought before arrival in London.

The Underground
- Eleven color-coded lines link 273 stations. Use a travel pass or buy a ticket from a machine (some give change) or ticket booth; keep the ticket until the end of the journey. The system includes the Docklands Light Railway (DLR; between Tower Gateway station and the Isle of Dogs). The Jubilee Line extension (Westminster–Docklands) opens late 1998.

Buses
- Plan your journey using the latest copy of the *All London Bus Guide.*
- A bus stop is indicated by a red sign on a metal pole.
- On a two-man bus, the conductor comes to inspect the travel pass or sell a ticket; on a one-man bus, the driver inspects passes or sells tickets as passengers board—try to have the exact change.

Taxis
- Drivers of official (mostly black) cabs know the city well. They are

obliged to follow the shortest route unless an alternative is agreed. A taxi is licensed for up to four passengers.

- Hail only taxis with the yellow "For Hire" light on; tell the driver the destination before getting in.
- Meter charges increase in the evenings and on weekends.
- Avoid minicabs; they may have no meter and inadequate insurance.
- Black cabs can be ordered by telephone: Computer Cab (☎ 0171 286 0286/2728/7272); Radio Taxis (☎ 0171 272 0272).

MEDIA & COMMUNICATIONS

Telephones
- Check the mark-up rate before making a call from a hotel.
- Use either coins or a BT phonecard from BT public telephone booths. Phonecards are on sale at post offices and news-stands. Some phone booths take credit cards.
- Information ☎ 192.
- Emergencies ☎ 999 (free) from any telephone for police, fire, or ambulance.
- ☎ 100 to check costs, reverse charges (call collect) or call person to person via the operator within the U.K.
- International telephoning: ☎ 153 for directory enquiries; 155 to reverse the charges.
- Beware of high charges on premium numbers—such as those prefixed 0839 or 0898.

Sending a letter or a postcard
- Stamps are sold at post offices and some newsstands and stores.
- Trafalgar Square Post Office stays open till late: ✉ William IV Street, WC2 ⊙ Mon–Sat 8–8.
- Mailboxes are red.

Newspapers & Magazines
- Quality papers include *The Times*, the *Financial Times*, the *Daily Telegraph*, the *Independent*, the *Guardian* and, on Sundays, the *Sunday Times*, *Sunday Telegraph*, *Observer* and *Independent on Sunday*.
- London's only evening paper, the *Evening Standard* (Mon–Fri), first edition out around noon, is strong on entertainment and nightlife.
- *Time Out*, (published weekly on Wednesdays) lists almost everything going.

Television
- B.B.C. 1 (varied); B.B.C. 2 (more cultural); I.T.V. (commercial—varied); Channel 4 (commercial—cultural and minority interest); Channel 5 (commercial—varied); satellite and cable channels (mainly in larger hotels) include CNN, MTV, and Sky.

EMERGENCIES

Sensible precautions
- Do not wear valuables that can be snatched. If you must bring valuables, put them in a hotel or bank safe box.
- Make a note of all passport, ticket, and credit card numbers, and keep it in a separate place.
- Keep money, passport, and credit cards in a fully closed bag. Carry only a small amount of cash and keep it out of sight.
- Keep your bag in sight at all times—do not sling it over your back or put it on the floor of a café, pub, or cinema. Keep an eye on your coat, hat, umbrella, and shopping bags.
- At night, try not to travel alone; if you must, either pre-book a taxi or keep to well-lit streets and use a bus or Underground train where there are already other people.

Lost credit cards

Report any loss immediately to the relevant company and to the nearest police station; also call your bank.

- American Express ☎ 0171 222 9633
- Barclaycard/Visa ☎ 01604 230230
- Diners Club ☎ 01252 513500
- Lloyds Card Loss ☎ 0800 585300
- MasterCard/Eurocard ☎ 01702 362988
- Nat West Card Loss ☎ 0113 2778899

Medical treatment

- E.U. nationals and citizens of some other countries with special arrangements (e.g., Australia and New Zealand) may receive free National Health Service (NHS) medical treatment. Others pay.
- If you need an ambulance ☎ 999 on any telephone, free of charge.
- National Health Service hospitals with 24-hour emergency departments include: University College Hospital ✉ Gower Street (entrance in Grafton Way), WC1 ☎ 0171 387 9300; Chelsea and Westminster Hospital ✉ 369 Fulham Road, SW10 ☎ 0181 746 8000.
- Private hospitals, with no emergency unit, include the Cromwell Hospital ✉ Cromwell Road, SW5 ☎ 0171 460 2000.
- Great Chapel Street Medical Centre ✉ 13 Great Chapel Street, W1 ☎ 0171 437 9360 is an NHS clinic open to all, but visitors from countries without the NHS reciprocal agreement must pay.
- Dental specialist: Contact British Dental Association ☎ 0171 935 0875 ext 222 for Helpline
- Eye specialist: Moorfields Eye Hospital ✉ City Road, EC1 ☎ 0171 253 3411; Dolland & Aitchison ✉ 229–31 Regent Street, W1 ☎ 0171 499 8777

(opticians and on-site workshop for glasses and contact lenses).

- For homeopathic pharmacies, practitioners and advice: the British Homoeopathic Association ✉ 27a Devonshire Street, W1 ☎ 0171 935 2163

Medicines

- Many drugs cannot be bought over the counter. For an NHS prescription, pay a modest flat rate; if a private doctor prescribes, you pay the full cost. To claim charges back on insurance, keep receipts.
- Drugstores open late include: Bliss Chemist ✉ 5 Marble Arch, W1 ☎ 0171 723 6116. ◉ Daily 9AM–midnight.
- Ainsworth's Homeopathic Pharmacy ✉ 38 New Cavendish Street, ☎ 0171 935 5330. ◉ Mon–Fri 9–5:30, Sat 9–4.

Emergency telephone numbers

- For police, fire, or ambulance, ☎ 999 from any telephone, free of charge. The call goes directly to the emergency services. Tell the operator which street you are on and the nearest landmark, intersection or house number; stay by the telephone until help arrives.

Embassies & consulates

- Australian High Commission ✉ Australia House, Strand, WC2 ☎ 0171 379 4334
- Canadian High Commission, Macdonald House ✉ 1 Grosvenor Square, W1 ☎ 0171 258 6600.
- Irish Embassy ✉ 17 Grosvenor Place, SW1 ☎ 0171 235 2171
- New Zealand High Commission ✉ New Zealand House, 80 Haymarket, SW1 ☎ 0171 930 8422
- Embassy of the United States of America ✉ Grosvenor Square, W1 ☎ 0171 499 9000.

93

INDEX

Citypack
London

While every care has been taken to ensure the accuracy of the information in this guide, time brings change, and consequently the publisher cannot accept responsibility for errors that may occur. Prudent travelers will therefore want to call ahead to verify prices and other "perishable" information.

ISBN 0–679–00013–5
Second Edition

FODOR'S CITYPACK LONDON

AUTHOR *Louise Nicholson*
CARTOGRAPHY *The Automobile Association*
                       RV Reise- und Verkehrsverlag
COVER DESIGN *Tigist Getachew, Fabrizio La Rocca*
COPY EDITORS *Celia Woolfrey, Nia Williams*
VERIFIER *Lucy Koserski*
INDEXER *Marie Lorimer*
SECOND EDITION UPDATED BY *OutHouse Publishing Services*

Acknowledgments

The Automobile Association would like to thank the following photographers, libraries and associations for their assistance in the preparation of this book.
© BRITISH MUSEUM 43 COURTAULD INSTITUTE GALLERIES 41 LONDON AQUARIUM 51 NATIONAL PORTRAIT GALLERY 38a, 38b REX FEATURES LTD 9 SCIENCE MUSEUM 27 SPECTRUM COLOUR LIBRARY 13b, 29, 32. All remaining pictures are held in the Association's own library (AA PHOTO LIBRARY) with contributions from: P. BAKER 7, 45b; D. FORSS 2; S. & O. MATHEWS 46b; R. MORT 13a, 18, 48b, 54, 61a; B. SMITH 24a, 24b, 30b, 35a, 40a; R. STRANGE 6, 23b, 25, 26a, 26b, 28a, 28b, 30a, 31, 44, 46a, 47, 49a, 49b, 50, 58, 60, 87b; M. TRELAWNY 16, 21, 42a, 56; R. VICTOR 23a; W. VOYSEY 1, 12, 17, 33b, 35b, 36, 40b, 48a, 57; P. WILSON 5a, 39, 53, 87a; T. WOODCOCK 33a, 34, 37b, 45a, 55.

Special sales

Color separation by Daylight Colour Art Pte Ltd, Singapore
Manufactured by Dai Nippon Printing Co. (Hong Kong) Ltd
10 9 8 7 6 5 4 3 2 1

Titles in the Citypack series
- Amsterdam • Atlanta • Berlin • Boston • Chicago • Florence • Hong Kong •
- London • Los Angeles • Miami • Montréal • New York • Paris • Prague •
- Rome • San Francisco • Tokyo • Toronto • Venice • Washington, D.C. •